DANCE
IN EDUCATION
by Rita Allcock
and Wendy Bland

DANCE BOOKS LTD
9 Cecil Court   London WC2

First published in 1980
by Dance Books Ltd
9 Cecil Court   London WC2N 4EZ

© 1980 by Rita Allcock and Wendy Bland

ISBN 0 903102 51X

Editorial and production by John Sanders Publishing Ltd, Oxford
Printed in Great Britain by Western Printing Services Ltd, Bristol

CONTENTS

Chapter 1

Introduction

Our decision to write this book arose from contact with many young teachers who, after studying modern educational dance at college, found themselves in difficulties when it came to putting their ideas into practice in a teaching situation. It is our belief that in many cases their lessons did not work well because the approach was too theoretical for the average child, that is, based too rigorously on a preconceived abstract 'movement theme' ('Today I'll do a dance on rising and falling, or meeting and parting'), with little opportunity for the children to make an immediate response to the dance stimulus from their own experience. The result is that too often the dance degenerates into a mere physical or movement exercise, with little claim to artistic content or expression. Rising and falling, meeting and parting, strong movement and light movement, dab, flick, glide, etc; these qualities may be exemplified, but one wonders whether the child is conscious of having taken part in a living, creative experience.

It is our belief that for too long these 'movement ideas' have determined modern educational dance in the classroom, and we feel that there is room and a need for an alternative approach, via the 'dance subject'. In practice, children often find it difficult to respond emotionally to 'dab' and 'flick', and unless the emotions are involved, the child cannot 'feel' the dance and will therefore tend to remain wooden, uninvolved and uninspired. The 'dance subject' is meant to bridge this gap—to provide the stimulus which evokes a personal response in the pupil, which is a prerequisite of a creative, as opposed to a repetitive and mechanical, sequence of movements. It follows that the 'dance subject' must relate directly to the child's experience, for only if it does so is the lesson likely to come alive.

In *An Essay on Man*[1], Goethe defines art as 'an interpretation of reality—not by concepts but by intuitions; not through the medium of thought but through that of sensuous forms'. As teachers of dance we must help to awaken these intuitions and spark off the creative process, expressed through the 'sensuous forms' of movement. Children should leave the dance lesson conscious of having taken part in something alive and exciting, perhaps not great art at this stage, but more than just a sequence of movements; aware, however vaguely, that their bodies have been used to express in dance some part of their own experience.

Our main aim in this book is to suggest to teachers possible ways of creating an environment which will encourage children to develop a personal involvement in the dance. This is achieved, as we have said, by selecting a suitable stimulus, the dance subject, with which the child can feel some identity and involvement. We give examples of lesson plans, in which dance subjects are used to stimulate the class to improvise. The teacher's main role is to encourage these improvisations and then to help develop the children's artistic judgement by getting them to select from their improvisations those movements which will form a pleasingly-structured whole.

The process we advocate is as follows: a *dance subject* is chosen which in turn suggests a number of more specific *dance ideas*. These are subjected in class to an *analysis*, in which the teacher and the class participate, which in turn suggests a range of *movement ideas*, and these are used in the development of phrases which provide the basis of the finished *composition*.

Dance subject

As we have indicated, our aim is to get away from the 'movement theme' as the basis for a dance and to use the personal experience of the child as our starting point. The first step is the choice of a general area of interest with which the children are familiar and in which they can feel some sense of involvement from the start, for example 'The Circus', 'Water', and 'Football'. These general ideas of interest we have called the *dance subject*. From them will stem a number of *dance ideas*, specific aspects of the *dance subject*, or associated ideas, which will then be used as stimuli for dances. These will be chosen for their action and motion possibilities, for the scope they afford for imaginative movement development. For example, 'The Circus', a dance subject for first years, is a complex, action-and-motion-packed concept including many different types of movement, like juggling and tightrope walking. These can be used as dance ideas, for example, the actions and movements of the tightrope walker will suggest movement material which will then be used as the basis of a dance composition. Dance ideas must therefore be relevant to the children's experience and stage of development, and must readily suggest a range of movement ideas. The circus, even if less frequently visited by children personally, is popular on television and our own experience is that this works very well as a dance subject.

Material connected with the dance subject, but chosen from other spheres should not be ignored. A poem or painting may prove a valid dance idea, a newspaper report or a piece of video-tape if available. In chapter 5 the poem 'Mushroom' provides a dance idea under the dance subject 'Growth'.

The teacher when choosing the dance subject for the lesson should take into consideration the movement characteristics of her class, the children's intellectual development and social and cultural background. We have given guidance on these questions throughout the following chapters, however we must stress that it is up to the teacher to assess her own class, to discover its particular problems and needs, and adjust her material to suit. For example, the stimuli she chooses should be related to the children's environment and experiences, which will in many cases be different from her own. It is of little value to choose 'The Sea' as a dance subject for certain classes of city children some of whom may never have seen the sea; much more suitable for them might be a dance subject such as 'Football'. Similarly introducing unfamiliar music to children who have only heard popular music presents problems which the teacher cannot overlook, unfamiliar music would immediately create apprehension in the children. This does not mean that, for instance, classical music can never be used with these children, but rather that the teacher must be aware of the cultural problem and introduce it carefully and gradually, helping the class to feel its way on this unfamiliar ground (see chapter 8).

Analysis

The analysis of the dance idea is an important stage in which the children are encouraged to 'think round' the idea with a view to discovering what kind of actions, movements and qualities are fundamental to its make-up, ie children and teacher discuss the dance idea in class. Observation and perception are important here. For example, if the dance idea is 'Wave Patterns' the class will need to think about the shape of waves, their pattern, how they build up to a climax, break and are dissipated; about the speed of the build-up and its quality, the nature of its breaking and so on. Another example of a less abstract dance subject would be 'Football', where the functional movements of the game, like kicking and heading, are discussed with the class. During the discussion the qualities and the shapes inherent in the actions may be observed and the class should be made aware of how they can be extracted from the real situation and converted into possible dance motifs. This stage of the dance process requires a degree of objectivity, a capacity for observation which is implied in the word 'analysis'. However, some dance subjects such as 'Creatures' or 'Moods' will require a more subjective and imaginative discussion in which the class may come up with ideas which had not occurred to the teacher. It is important to be flexible enough not to wish to force the class to develop one's own preconceived notions, and to be open to the possibility of unforeseen developments.'

Work with movement ideas as suggested by the analysis

The stage of progressing from the analysis of the dance idea to movement ideas is of paramount importance. If dance ideas were put into the dance as they stand in the real situation the result would not be dance but imitation: *being* jugglers, *being* a wave. The creative process would have been totally missed. As the analysis develops the class is encouraged to see the movement possibilities in the dance idea and to experiment and improvise with them. The analysis will have suggested these movement possibilities. With the help of the teacher the children rhythmicise, exaggerate, elaborate on their original movements in such a way that they have improvised a number of dance phrases. Rhythmic patterns emerge when accents and phrases are introduced into tightrope walking which together with devices such as exaggeration and repetition lift it into the sphere of dance. These phrases can then be elaborated by experimenting with different elements such as levels, directions and qualities. The qualities of the activity of tightrope walking are translated by the children as they work on the dance so that quick and slow movements on the part of the tightrope walker become qualities of suddenness and sustainment, sensations of urgency and excitement and sensations of lingering. The shapes of the tightrope walker in the circus ring are explored in a variety of situations. The position of hands, head and feet etc are analysed and used as a reference point. The result is a series of phrases drawn from the original movements which become the raw material from which a dance composition is evolved.

The analysis therefore suggests the movement material, the actions and qualities isolated by the analysis being then translated into images expressed in bodily movement. The movement experience of the children begins to come into play as the *natural qualities* of the stimulus (dance idea) find an analogy in *movement qualities* expressed by the body.

It is important to remember that dance ideas must be chosen which will suggest movement ideas which will reflect the movement characteristics of the year concerned. As the movement material is evolved and developed along the lines suggested, movement learning situations occur. Phrases are repeated, developed, improvised on, and ultimately a number of phrases and movements learned which can then be drawn together into a composition.

Composition

Under *composition* in the following chapters we give hints on the teaching of choreographic skills, perhaps the teacher's most important function. These involve selection of motifs, repeated, developed and varied to form phrases which are in turn varied and developed. Once these phrases have been clarified, ways are suggested for developing an awareness of the contrast and relationships which will evolve as the dance grows. Manipulation of this material results in clarity and structure of the dance forms.

Choreographic skills are of fundamental importance in all

dances: solos, duos, trios and group dances. From the improvisations and learning situations each child must be encouraged to use her imagination to select suitable motifs and phrases from which to build her composition. The teacher's role here must be to allow this decision, as far as possible, to be individual and to help the child to grow in experience so she will recognise and choose material suitable for the dance idea. Once the child, or group of children, have selected a number of phrases or motifs with which to work, the teacher can be more active as the chosen material (motifs, phrases) needs to be developed, varied and repeated as the composition grows. She should teach the meaning of these skills.

Repetition

The simplest use is to repeat a motif or phrase as it stands, creating patterns, such as a clown's 'funny walk' phrase.

Parts of the phrase or motif will be repeated during the composition, for example, part of the clown's 'funny walk' phrase, perhaps a big gesture, or the rhythmic pattern can be used in other parts of the composition giving form to the dance. Repetition is the first compositional skill to teach as it extends the material and gradually variation will occur.

Variation

Variation is change in a motif or phrase retaining some element of the original. The quality of fine touch could be varied to firmness or a change of accent might introduce syncopation to a flowing passage, thus varying the rhythmic content. Other aspects of the original might remain the same, or further on in the composition again, variation may occur, perhaps this time changing the spatial aspect. Sometimes there is very little difference between a complex variation of a phrase or motif and a development of the phrase into new material.

Development

This results in new material which is derived from the previous material. It may have grown from a fragment of the previous phrase such as the leg gesture from the clown's 'funny walk' which, previously hinted at, could be the important characteristic of the new phrase, and in this way relate back to the original phrase or motif. Development can also occur as a reaction to the original phrase, for example, after the clown's 'funny walk' phrase a tumbling phrase ending with the body held in an unusual position.

These skills must be taught from the start of work in dance and work on these lines is indicated throughout the following chapters.

Finally the teacher should be indicating to her class the key to their compositions, namely, relationships, one position to the next, one phrase to the next, one effort to the next. The contrasting or similar elements of movement are related to one another so as to give an overall balance, and when these relationships are repeated and developed, patterns are formed giving structure to the dance as tensions and climaxes are built and resolved. The teacher will help her class develop a kinaesthetic and intellectual awareness of how these relationships evolve by giving opportunities for observation of dances and discussion of the problems, and by working on solos, duos and groups.

In each chapter relating to a particular year-group we have tabulated a series of possible dance subjects. The table headings are suggested by the points just discussed, that is, dance idea, analysis, movement ideas. The development of these ideas is a matter for the individual teacher, but in the case of one of the dance ideas under each dance subject we have shown a possible line of development under the heading *Development of dance idea with teaching hints*. The aim is to help with the progression of thought from dance ideas through analysis and discussion of ideas and movement ideas to movement learning situations and finally the composition of a dance. These are meant only as possible guides, and it is hoped they will suggest to the teacher techniques and ways of thinking about dance teaching which she will be able to put to a personal use.

Chapter 2

Dance Ideas for 11–12 year Age Group

Dance ideas in the first year

Since our starting-point, if we are to involve the children fully in the dance process, must always be the child's own experience, we must be careful to choose dance ideas which are not beyond their intellectual, emotional and physical capabilities. Obviously it is pointless to expect from a group of first years the ability to pursue any great degree of abstraction in the preparation of a dance. The approach should be as down-to-earth as possible in the first instance, fully related to their preoccupations as eleven-year-olds and to their level of thinking and feeling. For instance, adults might approach the dance subject 'Water' in general abstract terms, talking about flow, transparency, reflection and buoyancy, whereas a child will associate it with a specific experience such as water games, or a waterfall on holiday. It is at this point that the dance teacher should begin, using this literal starting-point as a basis for creative work.

Moreover, for eleven-year-olds, the borderline between reality and fantasy is still rather blurred and this factor must be fully utilised by the teacher in the choice of dance ideas. The children will readily identify themselves with fantasy material and become caught up and absorbed imaginatively in it. The starting-point at all times is the child's own world, so that not just the body, but the understanding and imagination are involved.

It follows that dance ideas at this stage will introduce an element of fun and put to advantage the playfulness of first years, with all the spontaneity, gaiety and energy it involves (see the dances we have suggested on the dance subjects 'Circus' and Saint-Saëns' 'Fossils' from 'The Carnival of the Animals'). In their games, children of this age enjoy repetitive actions, such as jumping, skipping and hopping, in which the whole body moves as a unit. Suitable dance ideas will therefore often be playful and action-packed to cater for the movement characteristics of first years.

Movement characteristics of the first years

First years tend to throw the whole body into action, with gay abandon to movement, wanting to go and not stop. This exemplifies the quality of 'free-flow' in movement terminology[2]. The opposite quality of 'bound flow' which embodies a feeling of self-restriction and a holding-back of the movement is not natural to this age group. It should be brought in as a contrast and will need more practice than free-flow movement.

Most first-year movements tend to be large in both space and in body, with a feeling of suddenness and urgency rather than of sustainment or lingering. Girls can achieve the quality of fine touch with light and delicate movements more easily than robust, powerful, energetic movements which are generally preferred by boys. Sometimes the children will enjoy moving with a flexible quality, taking up as much room as possible, indulging in space along a meandering pathway. A contrast to this is enjoyed when moving directly through space.

Suitable dance ideas should therefore cater for these movement characteristics, but attempts will be made progressively to enrich the children's movement capabilities (vocabulary) by incorporating more 'unnatural' qualities.

An emphasis on solo work is necessary with this age group in order that the individual child should be responsible for his or her creative work. In this way the creative faculties of each child are stretched and there is no possibility of hiding in a big group. As a contrast, duo and trio work may be introduced in which the child discovers other children's capabilities and learns to work creatively and harmoniously with others. Large group dances are too overwhelming in their complexity for first years.

Composition

At first, dance ideas, should be kept as simple as possible, leading to short phrases and short dances, since at this stage the development of material will necessarily be limited and children will have difficulty maintaining the quality of their movement for long. They need to build up their compositions gradually. The tendency is for them to dance on and on with no thought for phrasing and punctuation. Consequently, attention to phrasing, the use of climaxes within the phrase and in the overall shape of the dance need to be taught, but over-complexity should be avoided. Initially, as few as two phrases may be used, and developed into a simple composition. This will result in a form which children of this age are able to understand and appreciate. It is vital to stress form and composition, simple though they may be at this stage, as a basis for future development.

The movement memories of eleven-year-olds are as yet untrained and their phrases are quickly forgotten, and this fact underlines the need for short, simple dances. The repetition of short phrases helps them to improve their movement memories and simultaneously to clarify the phrases. Variations on the phrase should then be encouraged, such as an increase in the *size* of the movement. This phrase-and-variation approach is a simple way of building a composition.

The importance of starting- and finishing-positions must be stressed, and indeed the teacher may find it necessary to suggest starting-positions to ensure a good initial relationship. It helps also if the children hold their finishing-positions in order to give the feeling of a finished product, that the dance has been 'rounded off'.

In duos the following relationships may be found useful: *mirroring*, ie the partners facing each other and mirroring each other's movements; *matching*, in which they match each other's movements; *question and answer passages*; *follow my leader*.

Trios can use the same techniques, plus circles, two-against-one situations and linear figures. The tendency for crowding often found in this age group should be avoided. This will be easier if the children are encouraged to be constantly aware of their partners' actions.

Music

First years should be given the opportunity to dance with music as well as without. Music will help clarify rhythm, phrasing and atmosphere. It is for the teacher to decide what sort of music is suitable for the particular class, depending on the degree and nature of their musical appreciation. Light classical pieces, such as Saint-Saëns' 'Carnival of the Animals', will usually prove appropriate, used either as direct stimuli or as an accompaniment for dance ideas (see chapter 8). Electronic music can also add greatly to the atmosphere of certain dances, and carefully selected items from the pop sector will bring a ready response.

Dance subject   Water

	Dance ideas	Analysis	Movement ideas
1	*Moods of water* eg *waterfall* solo	Turbulence, whirlpools and calm water suggest contrasting dynamic qualities; plunging, crashing, leading into swirling and eventual calm	Main stress: quality. Sudden, strong, explosive qualities with dropping leading into spinning and spiralling, fading into a light sustainment. Whole body involved
2	*Movement of waves* solo	Shape and pattern of waves, rolling, pounding, ebb and flow. Interest in rhythmic and dramatic pattern of build-up, climax and dispersal of waves	Main stress: quality. Interplay of sudden and sustained rising and falling with trunk arching and bending
3	*Rain* solo	Dripping, driving, heavy splashing, beating rain contrasted with drops bouncing on ground	Main stress: quality. Rhythmic content stressed. Percussive sounds with feet and hands. Fine-touch, sudden qualities build up through repeats to firm jumping and rebounding into different directions

Development of dance idea no. 1 with teaching hints

Discussion of dance idea
Pictures of water scenes could greatly help in stimulating the class's ideas.

Work with movement ideas as suggested by the analysis

1   Stand high on toes, rushing forwards and ending low.
       This requires a feeling of poise, stretch and stillness at the
       beginning, then freely-flowing, cascading down to a low
       level. Work on carefree, rushing quality.

2   Repeat phrase above adding turning and spinning at the end
(phrase 1).
       Whirlpool needs to flow smoothly from the drop and may
       rise and fall with turning. Encourage children to end this
       phrase rising so as to lead naturally back to starting position.

3   It may be necessary to practise spiralling to achieve satisfac-
torily increases and decreases in speed.
       By whipping the body round into turning jumps—by be-
       gining a spinning movement in the arm, which is taken up
       by other body parts so that the movement spreads, eventu-
       ally using whole body, then gradually diminishing.

4   A calmer effect for contrast and relief is introduced (phrase 2).
       Encourage the feeling of a light sustained quality: travel-
       ling with gliding, sliding, spreading of the whole body
       sometimes close to the floor.

5   It may be necessary also to practise leg gestures, involving
curving, turning movements.
       Try to encourage the use of legs in different areas round
       the body.

Composition

1   Selection of material: From exploring the above movement
ideas (given as possibilities), the children should be asked to select
movements and put them together to form a dance. At this stage,
many will allow the composition of their dance to be determined
by the natural progression of the waterfall, ie cascade–turbulence
–calm. The more imaginative ones may choose to abstract the
movement ideas suggested by the waterfall's moods and group
them together in a way which seems pleasing to them, without
being hidebound by the progression of these moods in nature.
They avoid any possibility of 'being' a waterfall by abstracting
and interrelating the shapes and qualities drawn from the
analysis. This should be encouraged.

2   Guidance can be given at this point, aimed at improving the compositions, by asking the children to consider the importance of a good starting-position and a satisfying conclusion. At this stage all that can be hoped for is that children can group movements they have selected into a *simple* form, for example, calm movements → turbulent, explosive movements → twirling movements → (possibly recapitulation of element two) → calm movements, dying away (that is ABC(B)A).

Dance subject   Circus

Dance ideas	Analysis	Movement ideas
1 Clowns solo	Tumbling, tripping, skipping, funny walks, upside down, unexpected things happening	Main stress: body. Involves isolated movements of different body parts. Sudden movements, stopping and starting, tipping over, use of exaggerated movements. Changes of level
2 Tightrope walker solo	Feeling of complete control and poise contrasted with tottering and suspense building	Main stress: space. Direct pathways with advancing and retreating. Body very upright, legs often bending to kneeling positions, rhythmical stepping and exploring with toes and heels
3 Juggling solo	Precision of timing as hands juggle with short rhythmic phrases, moments of suspense, constant movement of feet	Main stress: body. Use of isolated body parts. Head plays major role, focusing on movement of balls. Interplay of sudden and sustained movements

Development of dance idea no. 1 with teaching hints

Discussion of dance idea

Children will be able to offer many ideas of clown situations from their own experience. If music is used (for example, 'Popular Song' from Walton's 'Façade' suite, or 'Gaîté Parisienne' by Offenbach), this may suggest further ideas.

Work movement ideas suggested by analysis

1   Begin by working on a funny walk, a stepping pattern which has a character of its own, for example, toes turned out in a Charlie Chaplin walk.

This provides the beginnings of a phrase.

2   Exaggerate the movement, with introduction of a simple rhythm, for example, slow, slow, quick, quick, slow, with stops and repeats (phrase 1).

This will begin the transition from action into dancing.

3   Following phrase 1 above, another movement idea can be introduced (phrase 2), for example, a running jump with legs pedalling in the air.

The quick movements must be danced with a feeling of urgency in the body.

4   They now have two phrases which they can use as the basis for the simplest of dances, with music, if used.

5   Other possibilities for phrase 2:

Head peeping through legs, hands gesturing through legs; body held in unusual position after tumbling and so on.

Time should now be taken again to listen to the music, if used, listening carefully for musical phrases which can help the shaping of the dance phrases.

Composition

1   Selection of material: the class will be limited to two phrases which they can alternate and organise in their own way. Such a limitation is necessary at this stage for most groups. More advanced groups may wish to add phrases related to the dance idea. Dances should be short.

2   This dance lends itself to solo work which is vital at this stage to develop each child's creativity. There are no passengers in solo work.

3 Simple variations within the phrases enrich the form of the dance, for example, dancing the phrase in a higher or lower level than that for which it was composed originally.

Dance subject   Creatures (imaginary)

	Dance ideas	Analysis	Movement ideas
1	Air creature vs earth creature solo or duo	An airy undulating, contrasting with an earth-bound, foraging, and the metamorphosis between the two	Main stress: quality. Light, freely-floating, turning jumps, dipping and diving, then a transition to strong, bound, twisting, with joints of body in angular shapes
2	Large creature trio	Bulky form with weird writhings, contracting and swelling	Main stress: body. Twisting and turning, with linking of limbs. Travelling, keeping in the group, perhaps using limbs for unusual purposes, eg legs high, arms supporting. Group extending, contracting, revolving
3	Overheard on a saltmarsh. A poem by Harold Monro: 'Nymph, nymph, what are your beads?' duo	Duo with clear question and answer situation – a pleading, grasping creature encounters a deliberate barrier	Main stress: body. Clear gestures with firm, scooping upwards for pleading, knees and hands stressed. Flexible, sudden gathering gestures for grasping – rhythmic changes within the phrases. Linear body shapes forming barriers in space for refusing creature

Development of dance idea no. 1 with teaching hints

Discussion of dance idea

Encourage children to think beyond ordinary animals to imaginary creatures involving a new way of travelling, using limbs for unusual purposes. Suitable music for background may help stimulate the imagination, for example, Stravinsky's 'Firebird Suite' or certain pieces of electronic music. One can discuss also the contrast between the creatures.

Work with movement ideas suggested by analysis

1   Air creature

Lesson 1

(a) Hovering on spot, then travelling with jumps, back to hovering.

It is necessary to *feel* high; keep arms spread, flexible, held with head tilting freely, as it is important to keep moving slightly to hover. Hips should be helping to lift the body so that legs have minimum contact with the ground.

(b) From hovering into dipping and diving towards ground then soaring back up, sometimes straight pathways, sometimes turning.

The head can tilt the body over into the swoop down, travelling near to ground, then lifting back up, keeping a light tension all the time.

(c) Develop a short dance using phrases (a) and (b).

2   Transition from air to earth creature

The class, from hovering, sink slowly towards the ground, increasing in firmness as the bound creature takes over.

They can be talked through the transition, being encouraged to *feel* the increase in tension from a fine touch feeling to bound firmness. Unusual body shapes should be encouraged and one of these shapes should be held at the end of the transition.

3   Earth creature

(a) Changing body shapes (i) sudden changes, then freezing, (ii) more lingering movements, gradually coming to a stop.

This constitutes one long phrase, with contrasts in timing,

the sudden, jerky motif followed by a slow, menacing motif. Body is constantly changing shape, but there should always be firmness about the shape, stressing angularity with elbows and knees.

(b) Add travelling to phrase (a).

The irregular timing of sudden, then more sustained, movements plus the unusual shapes should create unusual methods of travel. It may be necessary to bring in jumping within the body shapes if the class is getting stuck on the grovelling movement.

4 **Transition from earth to air creature**

(a) One body part, for example, a hand, is released into a finer tension and moves more freely, undulating, lifting. This gradually spreads throughout the body as it rises back into hovering.

Again the class should be talked through the gradual release of tension and change of shape making them aware of different parts of the body as they change over.

Composition

1 Selection of material; there are two distinct ideas, an air creature and an earth creature, and the class have explored the movement ideas associated with both. Now they should be able to use these ideas in composing a duo. They need a starting position which clearly shows their relationship to each other, for example, both air creatures or both earth creatures, or one air creature and one earth creature. Their finishing position should likewise be held to show their relationship.

2 At this stage they need guidance to help their relationship and there should be discussion of the possibilities, for example:

(a) Earth creature captures air creature.

(b) Air creature influences the earth creature who joins her for a journey through the air.

(c) They influence each other and finish by changing places.

3 They should be encouraged to stick to the short phrases they have evolved during the lesson. They should watch each other and not always be moving at the same time, but try to develop a mutual awareness. This could start a question and answer situation influencing the form of their dance. In such a situation, the children should be made aware that their 'answer' can be contrasting with or similar to the question.

Dance subject The music 'Fossils' from Saint-Saëns' 'Carnival of Animals'

	Dance ideas	Analysis	Movement ideas
1	*Skeleton and ghost* duo music—close relationship	Sharp, staccato movements, brittle, very rhythmic following phrases in music (skeleton) flowing, undulating (ghost)	Main stress: quality and body parts. Sudden, bound movements with joints and angles of body. Then freely-flowing central trunk movements leading into spiralling turning
2	*From bones to flesh* solo music—close relationship	Isolated disconnected movements gradually drawn together and related, contrasted with bulbous, smoother movements as flesh covers bones	Main stress: body. Each part of body used separately in a sudden way, gradually linking up first limbs then whole body. As music changes, each body part moves in a flexible way, again gradually linking up limbs, then whole body
3	*Music used for dance study*	Strong powerful chords give way to brittle, hollow sounds in short rhythmic phrases. A flowing passage follows adding smoothness as a contrast	Main stress: body. Leg gesturing into rhythmic step patterns following closely the rhythm and phrasing of the music. Joints of legs are emphasised within the sudden and sustained stepping

Development of dance idea no. 1 with teaching hints

Discussion of dance idea
In this case, the class will listen to the music and be encouraged to feel the rhythm 'within themselves', by moving slightly as they are sitting around the tape recorder. The contrasting qualities in

the music can be made clear to them. The music and the dance ideas are both light-hearted and, in the discussion, the children should be asked for ideas on how a skeleton and ghost would dance!

Work movement ideas suggested by analysis

1 Skeleton dance

(a) Put the music on and ask the class to pick up the rhythm or part of the rhythm with their feet on a zig-zag floor pattern.

There are moments of stillness which are important to break up short phrases.

(b) The rhythmic, jerky quality stimulated by the music can be taken up in other parts of the body and in the body as a whole, stressing angular body shapes, such as elbows jutting.

The whole body shape will be constantly changing, not just isolated parts of the body moving.

(c) The music will help with the balance of phrases in this part of the dance as short phrases are repeated.

2 Ghost dance

(a) As the music changes to a more sustained sound, the quality in the body changes. There are more central trunk movements and curved gestures of the limbs as a free-flowing sustained quality takes over, on the spot at first.

Gradually unbend the angular body shapes into more curved shapes which move in an undulating way (phrase 1).

(b) Travel on short curved pathways, sometimes turning and spiralling, keeping the free-flowing quality in the body.

This is the second phrase in the ghost music, and is quite short, so the pathway can be specific, for example, to one side, to the other side on the curved pathway, then turning, spiralling round (phrase 2).

(c) Music ends with repeat of skeleton music and children should repeat their skeleton dance.

(d) They should continue working individually until it is clear that they know the music.

Composition

1 Selection of material

The children should be given the opportunity to discuss with a partner their own ideas and if they wish to choose a different dance idea, providing it is related to the dance subject, they should not be discouraged.

2   Since the music is light-hearted, the following ideas could be used: the skeleton has difficulty travelling, the ghost finds it easy; either or both may be afraid of the other.

3   The clear musical form will help the children to create a clear dance form.

4   Initially, it is advisable to keep to simple duo principles, ie

      (i)   One versus one, each keeping to his own role

      (ii) One versus one, changing roles

      (iii) Two together, in which case they will change qualities together.

Dance subject   Christmas

	Dance ideas	Analysis	Movement ideas
_1_	_Journeys: The Three Kings, Shepherds, Joseph and Mary_ group music: 'Christmas Cantata' by Honegger (background)	Majesty and power of kings Humility and meekness of Joseph and Mary Simplicity of shepherds. Their pathways meet	Main stress: quality. Kings—upright, firm, sustained direct pathway Shepherds—sudden stops and starts in advancing and retreating steps. Joseph & Mary (duo)—light, gathering movements, surrounding one another, stepping on a flexible pathway
_2_	_Worship, glorification and joy_ solo	Reverence and humility contrasted with exultation, uplift and joy	Main stress: quality and body gesture. Sustained rising and sinking movements leading to strong leaping. Harmonious gestures of upward-reaching limbs.
_3_	_Carol Dance using traditional carols_ group music: close relationship	Traditional circular and processional formations echoing rhythm and form of carol	Main stress: floor pattern. Stepping patterns with leg gestures tracing out the pathway (floor pattern) derived from circular and processional formations

Development of dance idea no. 1 with teaching hints

Discussion of dance idea
Introduction of the idea of three groups of people travelling—
kings, shepherds, and Joseph and Mary—and of their contrasting
qualities of movement. Listen to the music, other possibilities are
'Fantasia on Christmas carols'—Vaughan Williams, 'Carol Symphony'—Hely Hutchinson.

Work with movement ideas suggested by analysis
1 Start with a rhythm which could come from the music you
intend to use. The rhythm is picked up by the children in their
feet and taken into travelling.
> Keep the phrase short and clearly accented.

2 The children should have an opportunity to experiment with
the different qualities of the characters in the dance, using the
set rhythm as a framework.
> By adding rhythm to the travelling, one is dancing rather
> than moving.

3 Selection of characters:
> (a) Kings—firm, powerful stepping along a direct pathway
> with body held in an upright, majestic manner.
> Firmness requires strong tension in the body.
> (b) Shepherd—sustained stepping with sudden pauses, advan-
> cing and retreating, the centre of the body pulling back and
> contracting against the advancing steps to show caution.
> There are conflicting pulls in the body. This is a technique
> which will need practice.
> (c) Joseph and Mary—duo. Light stepping on a curving
> pathway with arm and leg gestures surrounding partner.
> Sustained movements with moments of stillness.
> The curving pathways can envelop each other resulting in
> a protective relationship.

4 Play the music as background to the dance improvisations.
5 Organisation of class:
Divide class into groups of ten (three kings, five shepherds, Joseph
and Mary).
> First years should be familiar with duo and trio work by
> Christmas. A group of five for the shepherds is the next

stage in group work as it results in simpler group relationships than fours or sixes.

Composition

1   Selection of material.

The three groups select their own travelling phrase from their previous improvisations. The resulting pathways will eventually arrive at the same spot.

> Through discussion the teacher can make the class aware of certain group patterns, involving pathways crossing, surrounding, meeting, parting and running parallel. At this point the teacher should give the children a chance to work without her guidance.

2   Each small group should know what the other two groups in their unit are doing.

> (a) Some groups travel quicker than others; they may arrive earlier or start later.
>
> (b) There can be different lengths of journeys.
>
> (c) Some groups may travel high whilst other groups are low.
>
> (d) Some groups may pause whilst other groups pass by.

3   The climax of the dance is at the point of arrival of the groups together (not necessarily arriving at the same time—some may feel that for realism Joseph and Mary must arrive first). This will complete the form of the dance.

Chapter 3

Dance Ideas for 12–13 year Age Group

In contrast to first years, second years are capable of showing more concentration and of pursuing a greater degree of abstraction in working with a dance subject or idea. They are more mature in their thinking, feeling and social behaviour. Group work becomes more harmonious, with all members working together independent of the teacher, towards a conclusion, see, for example, dance idea 'Witches' Sabbat', where trio relationships involve the group dancing in unison and travelling as a unit. They enjoy improvisation for a short time but quickly become impatient to use these in an actual dance. In fact the children show a greater involvement in the composition of the dance and therefore need more time than the previous age group to work out their ideas.

They have a need for order and pattern-making in their work; dance ideas involving a rhythmical approach, such as dance subject 'Witchcraft', and dance ideas involving shaping and design, for example, dance subject 'Visual Patterns', satisfy this need and have a simplicity in tune with the intellectual capabilities of this age group. Suitable dance ideas will also cater for the spontaneity and imagination which second years still retain.

Movement characteristics of 12–13 age group
There is an increased awareness of the shapes their body can make and second years are able to hold these in stillness. They are more aware of the gestures which their limbs make, for example, turning jumps, and should be encouraged to utilise this new awareness in an imaginative way, as in dance subject 'Creatures'. In order that the body may be developed as an instrument for dance the trunk of the body must be involved, linking the gestures

of upper and lower parts of the body and resulting in total coordination (without which the full expression of the movement is not achieved). The teacher needs to encourage this 'centre awareness' throughout her work in dance and it always merits special stress.

Second years have a liveliness and spontaneity in common with first years and enjoy dynamic movement. Their increase in body control means that they can change more rapidly from one quality to the next within the same motif, for example, fine touch to firmness. Preferences differ from first years in that the children are able to feel the quality of fine touch, sustainment or lingering more easily, and combine this with other qualities to form what Laban termed the *effort actions*—floating (sustainment/flexible/fine touch) or slashing (suddenness/flexible/firmness)[2]. The inherent rhythmic patterns within the effort actions are in tune with energetic second years. Towards the end of this stage they should begin to master the textures of movement, that is, combining effort actions and their inherent patterns in space, for example, dance subject 'Visual Patterns'.

They are aware of the variations possible within directions and levels and are able to remember and repeat these directional patterns, for example, the patterns they make across the floor as they travel in different directions, and also the patterns their limbs make in the air as they gesture. Clarity of gestures and of the shape the body makes both in travel and in moments of stillness is developing. They also have the ability to combine simultaneously body actions, such as spreading, with the quality of the movement, such as firmness (see the dance subject 'Creatures'). However, they still have some difficulty in combining all three aspects, body, space and quality and there is often a stress on only two aspects, for example, body and space aspects, or space and quality aspects, or quality and body aspects.

Composition

Dance ideas need to be very much involved with the shape/pattern/design content, and texturally rich in order to suit the movement characteristics of this age group. Dances should still be kept short as the pupils' ability to develop dance movements is limited. However they are able to develop their dances by using contrasting phrases; a first phrase may involve a firm sinking movement leading into a development phrase involving a fine-touch rising movement.

At this stage it is important for the children to be given help in creating dance motifs, that is fragments of movement which are distinctive in shape, body design and texture, which they will build into dance phrases thereby shaping and increasing the clarity of their compositions. They will still have difficulty in grasping the relationship between one motif and the next, but they do have the ability to compose motifs applicable to the dance ideas.

As we have said second years feel the necessity to complete a composition and through observing other dances they can be taught to appreciate the form of the dance, for example, AABA or AB or ABABC.

Solo, duo and trio work should be continued along the lines of the previous work but with emphasis on the development of duo and trio relationships as pupils in this age group are more capable of observing and reacting to the movements produced by others in their group.

Music

Music with clear phrases and a strong rhythmic content is useful to help children shape their dance, but a balance must be kept between music strong in dynamics and rich in texture to accompany dance ideas which stimulate the lively spontaneity of this age group.

Dance subject   Football

	Dance ideas	Analysis	Movement ideas
I	*Some skills of the game* trio	Kicking movements of the forwards, dribbling and advancing on the defence players who confront and tackle, prodding and probing for the ball. Shooting action of the forward is contrasted with defending leaps of the goal keeper to catch the ball,	Main stress: body/quality. Legs and arms gestures emphasised in thrusting movements towards and away from centre of body, interplay of sudden and sustained qualities. Use of different parts of the feet in dabbing, flicking and thrusting actions. Use of sustained positions as a

Football—*cont.*

		or diving along the ground outstretched or heading the ball. Positions held as in photographs	contrast. Goal keeper dives and falls firmly and suddenly with degrees of extension in the body
2	*Football crowds* group: 5 chanting accompaniment from the class	Group sway, swing and jostle up and down. Jumping up and falling back is contrasted with moments of watching, held in suspense, which explodes into vocal chanting, jumping, throwing or waving of arms in the air in excitement	Main stress: quality/body. Swinging side to side, contrasted with rising and sinking movements and series of sudden jumps up and down. Group jostles in close proximity to one another. Moments of pause held in body shapes perhaps, except for heads which could move from side to side in unison and with sustainment. A sudden contrast is made in arm gestures as arms are thrown into the air and waved around creating air patterns within the group. Whole bodies could be flung into the air as phrases of movement build to climaxes. Rhythmic chanting could accompany movement phases
3	*Characterisation of the referee* solo	Standing in authority, controller of the game, arm actions important, eg pointing finger accusingly, waving arms in disagreement and into clear directions. Shaking head and blowing the whistle. Dismissing players from the field with the power of command. This is contrasted with chasing the game and keeping up with the pace	Main stress: body. Series of arm and hand gestures involving thrusting, dabbing, flicking, slashing are built into phrases together with shaking of head. A contrast is made with travelling into different directions. This is punctuated by movements of pause and held positions in body in which designs in arms are important and a firm stance is held

Development of dance idea no. 1 with teaching hints

Discussion of dance idea

Discussion needs to be geared towards stimulating ideas along the lines of the actions, positions and shapes in the body involved in the skills of football. Encourage such suggestions to come from the children in the light of their observations of football games, by using pictures, newspaper cuttings or films as stimuli for discussion. Pursue the idea with the children describing the qualities which they observe in the football actions and the body shapes created by the players as they perform the various skills of the game, for example, firm, penetrating attack at goal with the body advancing and determined, or confronting defence, or the surging force of the goalkeeper's leap upwards with a thrusting quality, and the powerful extension in his body as he tries to save the goal. It is important that the teacher guides the children's observations and analyses of the skills involved towards their aesthetic aspects, rather than their functional and practical, aspects. By focusing on the aesthetic aspects, the essence of the actions is seen as pure qualities and forms which could have significance in the context of a dance. The qualities can be abstracted and freed (by using the imagination) from their practical 'football' situations, to be transformed into artistic elements which are ready for use in the dance composition.

Work with movement ideas suggested by analysis

1 Introduce a kicking action in the legs as in, for example, a penalty kick. Suggest that the kick is mimed by the children, so that they begin still, weighing up the ball in relation to the goalkeeper and the goal, then run to the ball, pause for a moment and kick through to score.

The kicking action has a thrusting quality carried out mainly by the leg and foot, which swing through to lift and direct the ball into the goal. Both preparation into and recovery from the kicking action are light in tension, but the moment of contact between foot and ball—the action, is firm and sudden, and creates a strong accent in the middle of the swinging action. The body shape needs to be compact and determined to succeed, leaning forwards with all energy directed towards a clear goal.

2   Suggest that the children repeat the action a number of times in order to set up a rhythmic pattern and clarify it.

The class need to be given time and opportunity to feel the swing rhythm repeated, the recovery of one swing leading into the preparation of the next. The teacher also needs to draw the children's attention to the transition made between repeated kicking actions because it is not easy to repeat continuously the swinging of the leg without the movement becoming monotonous. If an extra step or jump is added, the rhythm becomes more interesting to perform and to observe. Also, experimenting with transitional steps and jumps can facilitate the process of transformation from the practical kicking action to the dance motif.

3   Suggest that a variation is made with the phrase of repeated kicking actions by using another part of the body, for example, the swinging kick of the leg could be transferred to the arms or just the trunk of the body.

The rhythmic content of the phrase could be endorsed by vocal accompaniment, such as 'football-fans' chanting, with repetition of a 'preparation—accent on the action—recovery' rhythm, elaborated by step or jump transitions and varied in the part of the body performing the action. Phrases can be organised and shaped by climaxes as a result of acceleration in speed or increase in firmness or size of movement. These changes can also be seen as simple variations of the original kicking action.

4   Further variations of the mimed action can follow in order to transform the action into a dance motif. Encourage the children to experiment with variations on the movement to involve not only emphasis on using other parts of the body but also variations in rhythmic content. They may use pauses and different placing of accents and yet retain, perhaps, the firm—sudden qualities of the accented movements. The pupils should also experiment with variations in quality, in which the action could become one of fine-touch with a sudden—light accent being placed in the middle of the swing.

This should also involve changes in direction so that kicking—swinging movements are being performed not just forwards and backwards, but also from side to side or diagonally across the body.

5 Similar work can be carried out on other football skills, a goalkeeper's defending leaps, dives and falls.

Encourage experimentation in the use of the body in which contrast between isolated movements such as small heading movements, butting, can be made with the whole body movements, such as in diving along the floor with the body outstretched and arms fully extended above the head.

At this stage improvisations should have been created on at least two contrasting football skills.

Composition

1 Suggest that each child selects at least two contrasting skills, previously improvised upon and transformed into dance motifs as illustrated above. Suggest to the children that they perform the motifs (A and B) one after the other, sometimes repeating motifs. Help the class to build these motifs, interplayed and repeated, into phrases (A and B) which are shaped by climaxes, for example, a repeated 'kicking' motif A, with a rhythmic stepping transition section between the repeats, could build in size of movement to involve jumping and travelling forwards and backwards, thereby shaping the whole phrase (A). A contrasting motif (B) concerned with heading movements could be introduced as a basis for a second phrase (B). The two phrases could then be organised in any way, and partial or whole phrases repeated in any order.

The classical tertiary form of AABA could be tried as a class exercise and as an example of a form which is complete in itself. From this example each child could create his individual form by manipulating the material in the phrases, organising and restructuring it.

2 Introduce group work in which each group selects its own two phrases A and B from the work done previously by its individual members. Suggest that each group performs the movements in unison.

Group shapes will begin to emerge as the phrases are repeated in unison, and it is the task of the teacher to help the groups clarify these shapes. The shape can do much to enhance the character of the motif. For example, if the motif is one of leaping with a butt of the head, as in jumping to head a ball, the group could in fact create a phrase in which its overall shape is pyramidal with one person in the middle jumping high, and the other two rising in a lower level (but not jumping) yet retaining the gesture of the head.

3 Introduce a rhythmic variation of moving in canon as well as in unison. The example just given lends itself easily to this, and it can be appreciated how interest and exhilaration is increased if varied rhythmic patterns are created. In the above example the head gesture could occur in canon through the group or even be syncopated.

4 Encourage travelling of the group within the phrases and changes of direction of the group as it moves. Travelling could develop by one dancer leading the other two, or the trio travelling as a group.

Changes of direction and movements of travelling should be consciously used in the composition to enhance the dance motifs, and situations created which could be abstracted from the football game itself.

5 Work on selection and clarity of floor patterns which again endorse the dance expression and develop when travelling occurs.

Floor patterns could also be abstracted from situations which often arise in the game itself.

6 Each group should, at this stage, have two clearly defined phrases A and B which are contrasting, clear in qualities, air and floor patterns, body shapes, group shapes and rhythmic patterns. Variations through repetition need to be introduced in the group work and help needs to be given towards mastering transitions between phrases and parts of phrases by the group. Any number of simple variations, some of which were experimented with earlier, can now be incorporated in the trio composition.

Emphasis should be placed upon each trio achieving a clear form in their dance. The dance should feel as if it flows from build-ups in forces and tensions between dancers into resolutions in group relationships and further building. The composition should ebb and flow as the trio dance through the phrases they have created. Sometimes the group is in unison, sometimes in canon, sometimes one is leading the other two, or one is dividing the other two. Alternatively, the group could form circular group shapes which travel or spiral, break and interweave to reform again. Depending on the aspects of the dance idea upon which the trio have selected to concentrate in their composition, certain group shapes,

rhythms, and motifs, will emerge and certain others be rejected.

The trios have not as yet extended their material and skills by
using development, although there may be some groups who
attempt this of their own accord. The teacher needs to help
these groups to use development fully to extend their ideas
and material. It may be sufficient for the other groups to
concentrate on organising, arranging and structuring their
two contrasting phrases and variations, and their group relationships into a satisfying form for them. Experiences learnt
individually in paragraph *1* of this section will facilitate this
group task.

7 Having completed the composition, each trio should be given
ample opportunity to perform their dances several times in order
to refine and perfect the finished dance. The moment of performance in front of others should follow, so that each trio has the
opportunity of gearing itself up to dance in front of an audience
and of making the dance work artistically for themselves and their
audience. Everyone should also have the opportunity of observing the work of others, of learning to aesthetically appreciate the
compositions and develop the skills essential for critical appraisal
of the dances as works of art in the broadest sense.

None of this can be achieved without the teacher's aid, and it
is at this stage that discussions held between performers, watchers
and teacher could be so fruitful for developing a greater understanding of dance as an art form.

Dance subject   Weather

	Dance ideas	Analysis	Movement ideas
1	*Weather report* trio	Singing of winds, drumming of rain, swirling snow, radiating sun—all different aspects of weather which can be con-trasted to create 'changeable' phrases within a composition	Main stress: body. *Rain* drumming fingers on the floor, an incessant rhythm which is taken up by the feet, then the incessant rhythm broken by leaps from the floor *Wind* strong, flexible use of the body, bending,

Weather—*cont.*

swaying, splashing, spinning, gradually hovering to a stillness with a lighter tension
Snow   floating, turning, sinking of the body as a whole then slowly the body contracts into the centre
Sunshine   successive and then simultaneous spreading of the extremities of the body from the centre, followed by retraction back to the centre

2	'Wellies' (wearing Wellington boots) solo music: 'Raindrops Keep Fallin' on my Head'—soundtrack from 'Butch Cassidy and the Sundance Kid' (background)	Cavorting, heavy-footed clomping about, springing from puddle to puddle, kicking and splashing	Main stress: body. Exaggerated comic leg gestures, rhythmical stepping and leaping, turning with firmness, clicking heels, emphasising feet and knees, rest of body complements
3	Stormy solo music: 'Polovtsian dances' Section 3—from 'Prince Igor' by Borodin (close relationship)	A gradual rumbling as the storm grows, swirling, surging, threatening into flashing and cracking, dispersing and being tossed in the wind	Main stress: quality. Phrases of slashing with turning jumps; thrusting gestures of different parts of the body away from the centre, slicing through the air, contrasted with a lighter tension as body is tossed into different directions

Development of dance idea no. 1 with teaching hints

Discussion of dance idea

'Changeable' weather is a familiar term and an experience which all the class will have shared and be able to discuss. They might also discuss how sun shines through rain or that snow can follow sunshine. There is the possibility of the class making their own sound effects of the weather to accompany their dance, using a 'thunder board' for rolls of thunder or dried peas on a tray for rain effect. Records of 'weather sounds' are available and the class might wish to compile their own tape for their dance. They might also make the sounds with their bodies as they dance, for example, the sound of rain (by drumming on the floor with finger-tips) or even make the sound of the wind with their voices.

Work with movement ideas suggested by analysis

1 Rain

(a) Start the class close to the ground with fingers drumming into the floor for the sound of rain; there will be a lightness of tension in the drumming and the fingers will move very quickly with an upwards, downwards action. Exaggerate the up and down of the fingers—one hand at a time—so the drumming remains in one hand and the other is lightly lifted away from the floor in a rebound action that comes down to the drumming again whilst the other hand has its rebound action—like rain rebounding from the ground.

(b) The drumming rhythm continues as hands clap first against the knees, then higher up the body as the class rise to their feet and the feet take up the drumming—stepping on the floor.

(c) The drumming rhythm is broken by jumping away lightly from the ground, landing lightly with feet again drumming the ground.

The incessant drumming is characteristic of rain and is broken by the rebound action—again a characteristic of rain—to help rhythmicise the action. The body will be rising and falling with a feeling of light tension. A phrase should develop starting close to the ground with the

drumming fingers and going into drumming feet, ending
with the rebound leaps.

2 **Wind**
(a) The body travels suddenly, the feet skimming the floor and
comes to a stop. Sometimes the travel is quite long—to the
other end of the room—other times short. This 'rushing' can
come to a sudden end where the body is completely still, or a
more gradual end with the body 'hovering' on the spot; that
is, the body is not quite still but is slightly mobile with back,
legs, and arms, held with a light tension as if by a breeze. The
class could add the sound effect of wind 'whoosh' to this
rushing.
(b) The rushing can be first in one direction, then another, so
the class should work on what is their 'floor pattern' for this
phrase. They should change which part of their body initiates each movement; perhaps the wind blows their hips first
in which case they will move first in a certain direction and
as the body is tipped off balance the feet will quickly step in
that direction. Shoulders, head, an arm, or even a leg may
lead a movement.
(c) The hovering comes in between the rushing, as gusts of
wind are followed by moments of near-stillness. There should
be a feeling of uncertainty—waiting for the next gust.
(d) The class should be able to feel an impulse which takes
them quickly from the spot and then gradually slows down to
hovering. Impulsive movements have a very sudden start and
this is followed almost immediately by a gradual slowing
down. The class could spend time feeling an impulse in their
hands and arms before taking it into the whole of the
body.

> 'Impulsive' movements are rather sophisticated for this age
> group so try not to spend too long on this part of the lesson.
> Keep the gusts quite short and make the floor patterns clear
> so that the class knows exactly in which directions they are
> travelling. Again there will be a light tension in the body
> and the class will be travelling and stopping.

3 **Snow**
(a) A 'soundless' floating—this age group should be able to
'feel' the quality of floating, their limbs, trunk and head
free in the air as if no effort is required to hold them there. A

feeling of light tension throughout the body as it moves in a flexible way through space.

(b) Develop a motif which starts high with floating, slowly turning and sinking to the ground, ending with a 'melting', ie the finger-tips and the head curl in towards the centre of the body; this curling continues throughout the body ending with stillness and the body in a tight ball shape.

(c) The floating can be danced travelling from the spot, but make it clear that there should be no sound at all; just as snow is silent, therefore, they must be very careful about their foot-work—keeping it as light as possible.

It will be necessary to practice the quality of floating with the class, stress the light tension and flexibility of the body. They may do floating jumps with turns in which case their landings should be light and resilient.

4 Sunshine—again in silence

(a) Starting closed into the centre of the body there is a simul-taneous spreading movement in which both arms and one leg move away from the centre at the same time as each other until the body is spread; it then retracts back to the starting position ready to spread again.

(b) A 'spreading' phrase again, but this time the limbs move successively, that is, one after the other. For example, right arm (with right side), then left arm (with left side) followed by a gesture away from the centre by the right leg. The retracting can be danced successively also.

(c) These phrases of 'spreading sunshine' could be danced with a feeling of light tension or firm tension—either way is suitable to the dance idea and the class should be able to feel both qualities within this phrase.

(d) Build a phrase including successive and simultaneous spreading. One side may start and retract, then the other side retract, followed by the whole body spreading then spin-ning before retracting once more.

The spreading phrase is very concerned with movements away from and towards the centre of the body; it is the centre which initiates the movement and it is very impor-tant for the class to develop this technique.

5 Once the different ideas have been experienced give the class the opportunity to improvise in a solo dance. Before starting they

may decide what is their weather forecast. They will need to work on transitions from one phrase to the next—that is how the end of one phrase links with the beginning of the next.

Encourage them to dance each phrase more than once, for example, they may start with 'sunshine', go into 'rain' followed by 'wind' and 'snow' but end again in sunshine. Their dance will have moments of dancing on the spot and some travelling from the spot.

Composition

1 Ask the class to discuss in trios how they may use their own improvisations within a group dance:

(a) Each phrase could be developed by the three people dancing together, for instance:

(i) Rain—the drumming would be louder in a trio than as a solo; the rising and falling could be danced in unison or one could be rising as the others are falling or rebounding from the ground. This needs careful organising and the dancers would feel the relationship between them more clearly if they were close to each other, a counter-tension would develop within the trio as one sinks and the others rise.

(ii) Wind—again the 'rushing' into 'hovering' phrase could be danced in unison, in which case the 'rushing' would be more powerful. 'Hovering' could be in a rather closed group and an outside force (the wind) might cause the group to hover, facing first one direction then another direction before the 'rushing' starts again. This phrase might be danced with the trio in a spear-like group formation, ie one in front of the other two, or a wall-like formation (in which case all three would advance and arrive at the same time). A linear formation is also possible, one person being the leader and they may wish to follow each other, or first one go; she stops—then the next follows her and stops, and so on.

(iii) Snow—floating would best be danced individually at this stage. However, the trio could decide whether to sink in unison or one after the other, whether to float around each other or stay on the spot, and where to start and finish.

(iv) Sunshine—the successive and simultaneous movements

can be danced within the trio; a phrase might start with one person and she influences the others who gradually join in until the movement has been passed in a successive way throughout the group; or the group could dance in unison with a simultaneous movement. They could interchange these ideas as they wish. As the phrase is one of spreading and retracting so the group could start close together and spread away from each other then come back to a tight group again; once more this group idea might be danced either simultaneously or successively.

(b) The trio may decide to use the phrases to influence each other, for instance,

(i) Sunshine melting snow—in which case one dancer who has the spreading phrase will influence another with the floating phrase to start the curling into the centre (melting).

(ii) The rushing phrase (wind) may be directed towards the floating phrase (snow) causing the floating to swirl around.

(iii) The spreading phrase (sun) directed towards the drumming motif (rain) which reacts by gradually slowing down until it stops; this idea might be reversed and rain would cause the sun to stop.

2 Encourage the class to improvise as a group with their different ideas before finally deciding which ideas to choose for their composition.

3 They may wish to use their own sound effects or perhaps work out a weather forecast which could be announced as a beginning to their dance.

Dance subject   Visual patterns

Dance ideas	Analysis	Movement ideas
1 Shapes drawn on paper eg spirals, dots, zig-zag, stars. Children interpret their drawings with their movements	Spirals—spinning whizzing, either spring-like, or slowly unfurling, helta-skelta. Dots—pinpricks, spikey sharp. Zig-zag—sharp, angular, jagged. Stars—splintery, sharp	Main stress: space and quality. Spirals—sudden or sustained turning perhaps with change in level and an acceleration in speed. Dots—sudden angular—jointy movements, light in tension. Zig-zag—direct move-

Visual Patterns—*cont.*

	duo	dispersal of line. Pointed	ments with sharp changes of direction—angles made in joints of body. Stars—jointed movements contrasted with gestures contracting into centre of body and extending into different directions, a sudden light direct quality (dab) throughout
2	*Piece of newspaper, wallpaper or floor covering* solo or group (latter being linked to the pattern on material)	Note the relationship of shapes of patterns, colour and texture of material whether knobbly, coarse, smooth, silken etc. Use of repetition of design to create a pattern. Visual rhythms	Main stress: space and quality. Design and pattern stressed. Basic shapes, eg circles, lines, angles can influence the body shape, air and floor patterns, and can be combined with the qualities of movement, eg very dynamic design could result in firm, direct qualities etc. Repetition of movements in relation to repetition of pattern can be used. Rhythms of shape and quality created
3	*Photographs* eg geographical photograph of mountains or seascape, snow forms, sand forms etc rock formations	Dynamics of picture, eg strong or smooth important. Patterns formed, shapes and designs created within spikey, smooth, rounded bulbous undulating lines	Main stress: space and quality. Strong dynamic in movement can be achieved by combining angles and curves with rising and sinking actions and firm quality. All contrasted with lighter dynamics where fine-touch can be combined with curves and lines of less contrasting levels

Development of dance idea no. 1 with teaching hints

Discussion of dance idea

The teacher would do best to start with a picture of each of the 'shape-types' she wishes her class to be introduced to. Choice will depend on the children's needs in understanding shaping and interpretation of a visual stimulus in a movement response at their level. Some examples of basic shapes are zig-zags, spirals, dots, meandering curves.

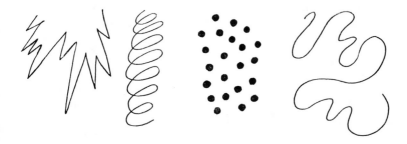

Show the pictures to the class.

As a possible stimulus for movement improvisation one could draw a verbal response from some classes by asking the children to describe what they see in terms of the characteristics of each shape. In many cases, where children are handicapped verbally, it may be best to omit this section or introduce it after a kin-aesthetic response has been made.

It is hoped that in this dance idea the children will have an opportunity of learning the relationship between seeing and feeling shapes or textures, and that pictures are two-dimensional and movement is three-dimensional.

Work with movement ideas suggested by analysis

1 Show each picture separately and encourage a movement response, for instance:

Spiral: begin the shape in an isolated part of the body, for example, fingers tracing out the shape in gestures around the body. The movement needs to be repeated gradually, so that more of the body is involved in the spiral, especially the centre, the movement becoming larger in space. A change of level could be introduced involving the body in spiralling low to the ground and spiralling high.

Fingers are used at the beginning because it is easy to produce the spiral as an air pattern in the fingers. The experience of the shape can then be transferred to the centre of the body moving.

Involving the centre of the body gives greater expression to any movement however small or subtle the involvement. The body becomes an instrument with which to produce a spiralling dance movement.

2 Spiralling naturally involves an opening and crossing of the body from the centre. Arms wrap around the centre, or open and spread away. This could be combined with high and low spiralling.

Variations upon this phrase could occur, for example, combining low/open and high/closed or vice versa as a result of spiralling; or relating small and large spirals, in isolated parts and all of the body.

3 Spiralling involves acceleration and deceleration of speed. This is now enhanced by introducing the qualities of suddenness and sustainment. For example, the movement begins low and sustained, gradually accelerating and rising, ending in sudden spinning and a pause.

An increase in tension could also enhance the spiralling phrase, so that one could begin with a floating quality which would gradually be transformed into a powerful sudden spiral, or a whipping or thrashing quality.

Spiralling involves flexibility of movement, the spine arching and bending with pliant gesturing. The teacher will need to encourage the children to use their spines in this way thus achieving clarity of shaping.

4 Dots: introduce as a contrast to the spiral. The dots could be introduced in the hands as if one is 'dotting' on paper. A series of sudden, light, directed pinpricks is the result. Transfer this texture to steps and jumps in feet and legs, toes performing similarly to fingers previously. An audible rhythm can be created.

Dot-like or dabbing movements are more easily felt in the extremities of the body. The joints of the body are pointed and better for sudden dab-like action.

5 Introduce a short phrase of dabbing involving the use of one or more parts of the body, for example, feet could begin with small gestures or taps which develop into sharp staccato jumping.

The phrase needs punctuating with the use of pausing:

dab, dab dab and pause

dab, dab dab and pause (A)

dab, dab, dabbing into jumping and pause after recovery. (B)

6 Introduce a third contrast such as the zig-zag to the children. Show the picture/stimulus, remind them of the descriptive words they used and respond to the stimulus in movement terms.

Encourage firstly zig-zag influenced floor patterns, stepping out the pattern with the feet.

This could be just a straight copy of the pattern from visual shape to movement shape.

A simple stepping rhythm could be clapped or spoken to enhance everyday walking bringing it closer to a dance movement.

7 Vary the length in the travel before a change of direction, and clarify the rhythmic patterns created.

Zig-zag patterns have an accent on the change at the points. This is seen and felt.

The accent could be enhanced by pausing before the change or jumping, gesturing or rising to a higher level, increasing speed. But to accentuate in movement involves combining light and strong tensions with suddenness. A light, sudden movement could result in light accents within a phrase of sustained dreaminess, and firm sudden movements, strong accents placed within a phrase contrasting in quality.

8 Introduce quality to the travelling. The zig-zag lines are straight and smooth. Perhaps the travel could be gliding with a sudden turn to change direction at each angle of the zig-zag, maybe with a change of level or a pause.

By clarifying the rhythmic and quality aspects of the travelling one is embodying an everyday movement—walking—with dance qualities to transform it into a dance motif.

9 So far the shape has only been traced in the floor pattern.

Introduce gesturing of limbs and body to form air patterns, using the phrase above in paragraph *8* after the pause, a gesture of any part of the body could complete the zig-zag pattern. Explore possibilities of 'zig-zag' gestures using one limb, two limbs, alternating, unison, one low, one high around the body, behind and to the side.

>The latter will involve a tilting of the trunk of the body.

>The body will begin to form angles using the joints of the limbs.

10 One could toss the zig-zag from joint to joint in short phrases punctuated by moments of stillness where the body is held in angular designs.

>This stillness will help the children to register the shape in their bodies kinaesthetically.

Composition

1 Observational powers are awakened in movement in the partner work that follows, and an intellectual contribution is asked for during the process of transposing the drawing into movement back into drawing and discussion.

The children are asked to draw their own pictures, remembering from the improvisations above, using the three shapes explored in movement situations.

>The teacher should suggest that the pen or pencil remain on the paper throughout the drawing except for dot-making. This facilitates relationships being created between the shapes. The children are now trying to relate visually into a satisfying whole the zig-zag, spiral and dots, bearing in mind their similarities and differences experienced kinaesthetically and perhaps verbally.

2 If verbal interpretation has not been referred to, this is a moment when the children should be called upon to describe what they consider to be the characteristics of each shape they are using ie what makes a zig-zag, a zig-zag and what is the significance of their zig-zag in relation to the other shapes on the paper? Is it larger, thicker and stronger, or weak and tentative?

>Verbal description gives further help towards clarity of thought and an intellectual contribution to the task.

3 Ask each child to compose a short dance stimulated by the characteristics of her drawing.

The dance and the picture should be greatly influenced by the earlier learning situations and resulting improvisations.

4 Encourage the transforming of visual shape to movement shape, visual rhythm to movement rhythm and so on, to be utilised at this stage to produce dance motifs. These, which are stimulated initially by the child's picture, have something to do with the characteristics of the shapes in the picture and their relationships to one another. For example, the zig-zag may appear dominant in that it may have been drawn large and thickly in relation to a tiny smattering of faint dots and a very thin, lightly drawn spiral. Or the spiral may have been drawn in such a way as to entangle the other shapes. Or a cloud of dots may give the visual impression of descending upon the zig-zag stars and spiral.

5 A dance motif needs to have sufficiently strong characteristics to have an impact on the compositional process. It requires richness and depth of content to become valuable in variation and development. It is the job of the teacher at this moment to judge whether or not a particular dance motif of the child has this strength.

Encourage repetition of performing the selected dance motifs several times in order to achieve the level of clarity of movement (characteristic to this age group) that the children are capable of producing.

Once the motifs are clear, the children can experience kinaesthetically something of what is contained in their motifs. The character of the motif will appear because the quality is stated clearly or the shape is clearly mastered in the body. The teacher needs to help technically with these problems, drawing upon her movement knowledge of how best to achieve certain bodily skills and qualities of movement (that is, working with movement ideas).

6 Encourage the children to complete a short dance whereby an overall form becomes visibly clear.

Repetition of motifs will need stressing so that simple variations, such as an increase in size of the motifs, can occur.

The dance should begin from some point, go somewhere and end in some place, not only in spatial and directional terms but in overall growth of the dance. An attempt at overall form, however brief, should be made.

7 Introduce partner work where one partner dances her dance whilst the other observes, having the stimulus, perhaps a picture, in front of her.

One is helping to develop the powers of observation for movement at this point and encouraging discrimination of the finished product.

A short discussion between teacher and partners could follow on whether the dance had succeeded according to certain criteria laid down by the teacher beforehand. For example, has the stimulus had any influence upon the dance or has the dance involved 'alien', perhaps favourite, movements of the child.

We feel it is valuable for the child dancing to have to defend her intentions for producing the dance she did, provided the teacher is not judging the dance from adult standards. The observers are also learning something about appreciation and evaluation of what is happening in the dance.

It is vital that this section does not become academically complex and abstract, but that it is kept at a simple practical level.

Dance subject   Creatures

Dance ideas	Analysis	Movement ideas
'*The Eagle*' by Tennyson solo	The poem emphasises the powerful tension within the eagle, a hanging power at the height to which he aspires. There is an interplay between clasping, watching and a sudden thunderbolt drop	Main stress: quality. Firm tension in sudden gripping movements contrasted with held positions of the body, fine-touch high and spread. This can gradually increase in tension which is contained in bound flow and sudden release in a thrusting drop
2 '*The Spider*' by David Barnes solo music: optional	Careful steps—delicate and poised in body. Gestures feel outwards from the hub of the body then a sudden recoil. The web design	Main stress: quality and body Light bound stepping, maybe tracing a weblike floor pattern. Moments of pause where the tension in

Creatures—*cont.*

	'Neptune the Mystic' from 'The Planets' by Holst (background)	could be traced with malicious care by the feet, followed by a cowering in stillness of the whole body and an engulfing of the entrapped insect	the body increases to firmness. Gestures extended away from the centre of the body with a fine-touch direct quality. This is compared with a sudden contraction in centre of body, a drawing of limbs to it. Maybe a sustained swaying following by a sudden firm grasping or snatching movement could be introduced
3	*'The Death Dance of the Whirley Gums'* A poem by Elizabeth Powell group music: 'Gnomus' from 'Pictures at an exhibition' by Mussorgsky (background)	A frenzied swirling 'Big Red Feet' tramping Grotesque creatures dancing wildly ending in twitching and jerking in 'fitful starts' as they loll and sink to death	Main stress: body. Running and jumping, twisting and turning of whole body. A build-up of speed with strong rhythmical stepping into spinning and stopping. This is contrasted with sudden sharp twisting gestures of joints as the body sinks gradually collapsing and becoming heavy

Development of dance idea no. 1 with teaching hints

Discussion of dance idea

Copies of the poem need to be distributed to the class, and the poem read aloud to the children. The interpretation of the poem will effect the tone of the work to follow and the mood of the dance. It should be read in a stimulating and vivid way. A feeling of loneliness can become real through the reading, and the solitary power of the eagle hovering above all should capture the children's interest. By emphasising the characteristic movements that the creature in the poem transmits, ie the essence of what makes an eagle, the bird we can describe to others, will lead more easily towards abstracting dance movements rather than mimetic copies of an eagle flying.

Work with movement ideas suggested by analysis

1 There are numerous ways of using poetry as a stimulus for a dance. What follows is only one possible way. The aim is to work towards performing dance motifs.

Spreading motif (A)

Begin by experimenting with spreading movements from the centre of the body through to the limbs. Begin with the body contracted in the centre, forming a ball shape. The spreading follows on the spot, limbs gesture outwards into a hanging shape, maybe slightly curved over. The spreading can be taken into a step.

2 The movement is one of dignity and power. Increase in tension spreads through the body as the movement spreads. The movement is dissolved and repeated.

> Dissolving the movement could be left to the class initially and then suggestions given by the teacher. For example, turning, stressing one side of the body and gradually gathering into a ball or contracting suddenly in the centre of the body bringing the body into a tight curved shape.

3 The spreading could be varied by introducing travelling. A series of steps each spreading the body a little more, or spreading to the fullest and travelling holding the open shape, finally dissolving the movement as suggested above.

> One is teaching the meaning of variation to the children.

4 Encourage improvisations on the spreading motif, for example, spreading in jumping, or from kneeling positions involving a lower level or changing the time factor, such as spreading suddenly or with the quality of sustainment. Successive spreading can result in a different rhythm.

> Throughout the improvisations encourage the quality of firmness—particularly by gripping and tensing muscles in the legs and hips, having a wider base and gripping the floor with one's toes.

> Motifs are beginning to emerge in readiness for the forming of the dance.

5 *Clasping motif* (B)

A contrast is needed. Focus could be upon the feet clasping and releasing (on the floor and in the air). A short rhythm could result, such as clasp-release, clasp-release, clasp and hold, using both or alternating feet, stepping into different directions.

Give vocal help with the quality of clasping—firm, sudden or flexible.

The release is a small, light scattering gesture with the legs.

6 Introduce the phrase in the poem 'He clasps the crag with crooked hands'. From clasping feet move to clasping hands. Experiment with the action of clasping and releasing in hands, then in other parts of the body, such as elbows, arms, trunk of body, and legs.

> Involving one's centre in clasping means a contracting movement and brings the clasping action into the main part of the body giving greater expression to the movement.

> One needs to remember that in order to clasp again one must release from the previous clasp. The release needs to be a recovery from the firmness of the clasp, that is, a fine-touch, opening movement.

7 Introduce the adjective 'crooked' to the shapes in the body being produced, and to the action of clasping in the hands and feet.

> 'Crooked' involves twisting movements in the trunk and limbs of the body. Limbs twine in and out of one another, knotting, and unknotting. The clasping action in hands and feet becomes more flexible. Bony parts of the body such as knuckles in hands, wrists, elbows, shoulders, hips, ankles, knees protrude into different directions one after another.

> The 'clasping with crooked hands' should be forming a dance motif. The spreading motif earlier could be used with a lighter quality as a release, building the two motifs into a phrase.

8 *Plunging motif* (C)

Introduce a new idea from the poem—'He watches from his mountain-walls, and like a thunderbolt he falls'. Improvisation could follow from the stimulus of the poetic image.

> A feeling of suspension, of light tension held high, could be experienced, followed by an attacking thrusting downwards of the whole body. The body shape could become more compact and facilitate the thunderbolt quality as a contrast to the spreading.

> This may help to avoid arms being used like wings.

> In the improvisations one is working on movement impressions which, once achieved, need to be shaped in the body and in space, for example, the impression of being

suspended which involves a combination of fine-touch and sustainment.

Allow experimentation on the part of the class.

It may help the composition to suggest that the suspending movement and the sudden drop are linked as one unit. Although there are two parts, suspension and drop, one is not complete without the other.

A change of hand-shape will help achieve the illusion of power; from clasping to a clenched fist in the thrusting downwards. Maybe the elbows could be emphasised in the movement and the body sink at an angle.

Give the children a chance to repeat this motif from suspension to drop, so that they may experience the changes of quality and clarify them.

Composition

1   Three possible motifs A, B and C have been improvised upon, and in some cases have been built into a phrase. Each motif has a strong characteristic, motif A a spreading one, motif B a clasping one, and motif C a plunging characteristic. These motifs could form the basis of a dance, and by varying, and developing them build up a dance composition. Encourage the children to produce variations on motifs, A, B and C, stressing simplicity of variation, for example, changing the level of the spreading motif or the part of the body in the clasping motif, or holding a clasping position in the whole body whilst jumping. Or they may change the quality of the action from strength to lightness (ie firmness to fine-touch) or from suddenness to sustainment, whilst retaining the shape of the motif in the body.

The latter variation is more difficult in that it demands greater bodily skill and sensitivity in changing the quality whilst retaining the shape, and even greater skill in changing the quality within the same action of spreading or clasping or plunging.

Repetition of the motifs will need to occur for the variations to take place, and with repetition should come clarity of motifs (to what degree will depend very much on the ability of the class).

2   Phrases can be formed incorporating motifs A, B and C and their variations. Encourage shaping of the phrases by building up

to climaxes and resolving them, highlighting some part or parts of each phrase by perhaps accelerating in speed or increasing in tension to the important movement, and then holding a pause or resolving it in some form of contrast.

3 Encourage clarity of the phrases formed so far through repetition.

> The children tend to have difficulty in remembering what they have produced. It sometimes helps to describe their phrases verbally for them as they try to repeat the phrases.

> It is important to remember what one achieves during composition, otherwise movements are lost.

4 Suggest to the children that they try to develop some of their material by taking part of a previous phrase, such as a transitional movement into a particular kind of jump or gesture, and repeating this, varying it and allowing it to lead on into new motifs.

> 'Keep dancing' is the key to developing new motifs. The small portion taken from a previous phrase will form the basis of a new motif which can be varied and extended to form a new phrase D.

5 To give the composition overall form the various phrases need to be organised in such a way that there flows throughout the composition a 'movement logic'; each movement is logical in thought, shape, texture, design in the body and so on. Encourage the children to organise their phrases into some coherent form in which each phrase leads on from the previous one either as being a repeat or as a similar phrase, or as a contrasting phrase.

> At a later stage the children will begin to appreciate the relationships created between one phrase and the next. At this stage they may be able to 'feel' what is right by repeating the composition several times.

6 Stress the performing of the dance compositions to the best possible standard that each child can achieve. Certain bodily skills needed for their compositions should be executed with a degree of mastery that allows fluency and clarity of the dance composition to develop.

> Each composition should be danced with a similar inspiration that stimulated the improvisations earlier. Some children may only remain at a mimetic stage of imitating bird-like movements, but one hopes that many will have grasped the import of the previous improvisatory situations and will

compose from those beginnings by abstracting the powerful
tension of the eagle.

Dance subject   Witchcraft

	Dance ideas	Analysis	Movement ideas
1	*Witches' Sabbat* trio music: 'Witches' Sabbat'— 'Symphonie Fantastique' by Berlioz (background)	Primitive worship of devil, hypnotic encirc- ling, then rushing to ensnare others	Main stress: body. Rhythmical circling step- ping pattern building up a simple repetitive rhythm, the body leaning forwards then backwards in a smooth encircling build to a climax and follow with travelling on a curved pathway
2	*Spellbound* solo music: 'Listen and Move records', a suitable electronic piece (background)	Rushing carefree, con- trasted with a restricted tightening sensation; a feeling of captivation to which one either sub- mits or fights against to break free	Main stress: body/space. Moving in a very free way with jumping and travel- ling gradually becoming restricted in the amount of floor space used, then restricted in space around the body causing a gradual withdrawal of movements into centre of body ending contracted; or scattering with free flow to travel on large circular floor patterns
3	*'Hist Whist'* *a poem by* *e e Cummings* solo or group	Very likely full of the unreal 'little ghost things' 'Twitchy'—'hopping', etc., have their own suggested movements whilst sounds in the poem can be experimented with, eg 'hist', 'whist'. Could be a dramatic dance	Main stress: body. Grotesque shapes which change sometimes sud- denly at other times with sustainment. Travelling 'twinkletoe', 'hoppy' etc have implied qualities

Development of dance idea no. 1 with teaching hints

Discussion of dance idea

Of all the aspects of witchcraft it is the sabbat which has attracted the most attention and there are many references to this subject in literature. The teacher may be able to draw on local legend during her discussion. A sabbat was an assembly of witches to worship the devil, but it took on many different forms, each sabbat holding its own particular rites. The sabbat was of pagan origin but was deemed heretical in the Middle Ages as witches were supposed to pay homage to the devil; there was often a banquet followed by dancing. One 'eye-witness' reports on dances which were performed in a circle, always to the left, frenzied, with hands joined and the dancers back to back. There are many interesting accounts of a sabbat, *The Encyclopedia of Witchcraft and Demonology* by Rossell Hope Robbins being particularly detailed. It will be necessary to keep the discussion limited to how it will affect the dance, and the class could relate a 'witches' dance' to what they have observed of other primitive dance rituals using repetition, rhythm, and dancing in a circle.

Work with movement ideas suggested by analysis

1 Start with a simple stepping pattern, such as forward (left foot) forward (right foot) back (left) back (right). Stress the first step forward and, for the rest of the stepping, the body accents the stress by leaning forward then gradually leaning back.

> A strong accent will result in a clear rhythm—in primitive dance repetitive rhythms were used to send people into a trance.

2 Introduce a circling sensation to the phrase, the head dropping forwards on the first stress and then slowly coming back and in a lighter circling movement. The stepping pattern will change slightly into a circling pathway but the rhythm will remain (phrase A).

> It is not necessary to teach the change in the pathway as it should happen naturally when the circling sensation is introduced.

3 Ask the class to work on their own with this phrase, starting slowly, gradually building up to a climax.

This climax could be achieved by increasing the speed or increasing the tension.

4   A smoother, gliding element is introduced as the class travels with large steps on a curving floor-pattern ending with smaller steps in a tight circle. The body is held with a feeling of light tension, the phrase flows freely and is easily repeated (phrase B).

> The witches are spreading and the curved floor-pattern is to ensnare others, hence the tight circle at the end. This flowing phrase will be a relief after the first phrase and the class should be encouraged to experiment with curving floor-patterns but use the tight circle at the end of each big curve to give definition to the pattern. A circling floor pattern has an innate rhythm, starting slowly and gradually increasing then decreasing the speed.

5   Ask the class to improvise on these two phrases, linking them together as they wish, and introduce the music to be used in the background.

Composition

1   The class should be grouped into trios to discuss the dance idea, relating the previous work to a trio relationship. They should realise why the phrases were chosen—the rhythmical, repetitive phrase as hypnotic, trance-inducing, and the smooth, gliding phrase for ensnaring other people.

2   Encourage the trios to use a circle formation as a dominant feature of their composition, the magic properties of a circle were important to witches (see initial discussion).

> The original phrases are suitable for a circle formation.

3   A further development might be to break from the circle formation. Some examples:

> (a) Using the gliding phrase (phrase B) the circle can break into a linear formation with a leader, ending in an ensnaring group.
> (b) Phrase B can be used to disperse the group as each member dances away from the circle. This can be done one after the other or all at the same time, or even one going, and then the other two together.

4   The floor patterns in phrase B can be used by the trio to develop their dance. They may have crossing pathways, and/or converging pathways.

With a trio this part of the composition could become involved and it would help retain clarity if it was kept fairly simple and not too set.

5   The trio should decide how to end their relationships. By referring back to the dance idea they should be able to find a suitable climax and conclusion for their dance, perhaps using the circle formation once more or ending dispersed.

Encourage individuality in the conclusion of their compositions, give the class time to discuss their ending and the reasons for their choice. Guidance should be given to ensure that the chosen conclusion will be a result of the rest of the composition, relating, perhaps, to the original phrases, or, the culmination of the 'Sabbat' with the appearance of the devil or the end of the 'Sabbat' when the cock crows.

Chapter 4

Dance Ideas for 13–14 year Age Group

The desire to conform to the rest of the group is of paramount importance in this age group. Their awareness of the relationships made between one dancer and another individually and in a group is greatly increased and dance ideas should encourage this, for example, dance subject 'Violence'. They are impatient to form the relationships right through to the end of the dance; sometimes at the expense of the clarity of the dance motifs. There is an advancement in their ability to work independently of the teacher which can be seen when they are willing to offer their own dance ideas. There is also an increase in their power of concentration, and memory, which enables them to reproduce dances previously developed.

This age group is beginning to lose the spontaneity children have and are more selfconscious. As a result they are less willing to improvise individually than previous age groups, needing to feel one of a group and, because of this, prefer to be given studies conforming to a set sequence of movements. Dance ideas should give a strong framework to satisfy this need without dictating the complete dance form as this destroys the creative work the group can produce, for example, dance subject 'Pop Star'.

At this age they like to discuss their ideas and are more objective in their criticism of other people's ideas. However, they can be oversensitive to personal criticism and need encouragement in order to feel a sense of achievement in their work.

With increased intellectual development should come the ability to abstract for themselves movement ideas from the dance ideas, which is vital if dance is to be an artistic experience rather than storytelling, miming or acting out emotions. The teacher must develop their ability to abstract as this lays the foundation for more advanced work in the future. Therefore, during discussion the teacher will share with the class her analysis of the dance idea and how the movement ideas arise from there.

Movement characteristics of 13–14 age group

Third years are able to show a degree of harmony in the way their bodies move. 'Centre-awareness' is greatly increased and should be encouraged so that gestures of the upper part of the body involving the chest area will be linked through the centre of the body with gestures of the lower limbs involving the hips. They are confident in the movements mastered, but feel uneasy with new movement situations and anything they consider to be an ugly use of the body. They are physically maturing at a rapid rate which results in a dislike of jumping activities, but they can understand and express elevation through rising movements without actually jumping. Rhythmic floor patterns are enjoyed and can be utilised as starting points for dance lessons.

This age group is able to combine all three aspects of movement, ie body, space and quality in the same action. Their dances will contain a variety of effort actions and they can easily change from one to another as can be seen in the following guides for lessons. They can cope with more complex rhythms and are able to translate the mood of music and painting into a dance context.

There is a growing awareness of the significance of certain actions and shapes in relation to the dance ideas. The limping movement in the dance idea 'Moon Dance' (dance subject 'Primitive Style') signifies the weakness of the new moon and there are other symbols in this dance idea. The pupils enjoy spatial actions such as rising and sinking, advancing and retreating because of their stability which gives them confidence in their own performance.

Composition

This age group is beginning to develop phrases and longer dances with more complex material and relevant variations which evolve logically. However, the overall form of the dance sometimes comes to an abrupt end or lingers on too long for, as yet, they may be unable to develop the material to its natural conclusion. This development comes at a later stage.

Trio work can be continued and an introduction to four in a group resulting in relationships such as two *versus* two; one *versus* three; or all four together. In groups of five they are able to create uneven relationships resulting in dramatic situations, as in dance subject 'Pop Star'. In groups of four this even number often creates a much more stable relationship, for example, dance idea 'Moon Dance' (from dance subject 'Primitive Style'). There is a stress on group work at this stage and they enjoy working on a group motif either by choosing one individual motif and copying it, or composing a group motif from a group task, again, see dance subject 'Pop Star'.

Music

Third years are becoming more influenced by the youth culture which, at present, makes it difficult for them to accept classical music. There is a good source of suitable music to be found in some 'progressive pop' or 'jazzy beat', such as Santana, Blood Sweat and Tears, Herbie Hancock and Pink Floyd. Music can be used as a direct stimulus for the mood of the dance, or the dynamics, or the rhythmical phrases as pupils are able to extract these aspects from the music.

Music plays an important part in helping more inhibited groups to dance, giving them a framework to their dance. A less inhibited group may prefer to work without music as they find the framework it gives is limiting. These groups will enjoy creating their own rhythmical patterns within the dance, for example, dance idea 'Bats' (dance subject 'Study').

Teaching of dance studies

A dance study is one of the many ways in which movement material may be presented for making dances. It presents a learning situation in which the children should achieve a degree of mastery and understanding of the given movements and underlying principles. Motifs, phrases, half-completed dance forms may be given, or even a complete dance choreographed by the teacher, all of which need to be mastered by the class. Movement and choreographic information is presented in a set form requiring very little creative work from the children, but total concentration on the mastery of the techniques involved in the dance study. Once mastered, opportunities must be given for creative use of these techniques by each child in the context of her own work.

The mastery of the dance study is not the end of study presentation but is a foundation for further learning situations demanding similar techniques. It is hoped that the movement vocabulary and choreographic skills of the pupils are increasing in each dance lesson and that the dance study is no exception to this.

For the dance study to be effective the teacher needs to perform the study well, for two reasons. Firstly, unless the movements are executed clearly and with quality in the body and orientated in space, the children will have difficulty in observing and grasping the point of the study to be experienced. The teacher will also have difficulty in repeating her study and the children in mastering it. Secondly, most third-year children have reached a stage in emotional and physical maturity when they want to identify themselves with adult behaviour. Observing and copying 'clumsy'-looking movements, lacking the poise and dignity with which the children wish to identify, is embarrassing to them. The children are very conscious of their own movements and will avoid embarrassing situations.

The pupil's powers of observation have increased together with a critical mind. Judgements for 'good' and 'bad' dances have developed and they are quick to notice a lack of body coordination or control in their own and other's movements and performances, particularly those of the teacher.

Inventiveness will sometimes be inhibited at this stage by a desire to belong to the peer group and to conform to the group norm. As a result of peer group pressures upon the children, creative work—in which individual differences of ideas and movements should be encouraged by the teacher—is not enjoyed as much as in previous years. Study presentation (where set sequences of movement are given to be mastered by the class) can remove many of the uncertainties from the more creative learning situations and is, therefore, a valuable method of presenting dance material in the third-year teaching programme.

Mastery of the study is not, however, the ultimate aim; a study, as stated earlier, is a learning situation from which the newly mastered techniques and choreographic skills are transferred to a more creative situation. It is imperative for the teacher to help children to keep alive the 'creative spark' (so vital for later work) through this difficult adolescent period. This is possible to achieve by valuing and rewarding creative work on the part of the children and encouraging and fostering it through such dance ideas as 'Worship of a Pop Star'. It is evident, therefore, that a balance needs to be maintained between creative and study work with the stress coming perhaps on the study presentation first.

Composition of a study

A teacher sensitive to the climate of her class will, at the appropriate time, coax the children into more creative work using the information learned in the study. One way of achieving this, for example, is to present a dance study, maybe only a phrase of movement (phrase A) which uses gliding arm gestures and gliding steps involving much sustainment. The class master the study, then are asked to create a variation on the study phrase changing the sustained quality to suddenness—thereby creating an acceleration in time-changing gliding to dabbing, or changing the levels of the movements.

A second phrase (B) could be created by the children in which a contrast to the given study phrase is achieved by the direct quality of gliding being changed to a flexible quality (thereby making a subtle transition from gliding actions to floating actions). Or the fine-touch quality in the gliding action might be changed to firmness in a pressing action. If all qualities of directness, sustainment and fine-touch in gliding are changed to their opposites of flexibility, suddenness and firmness, a sharp contrast is achieved and a more obvious transition made from the gliding actions to those of slashing.

Phrase B would, therefore, be a variation of the given phrase, and an experience in manipulating material and mastering one of the compositional skills, such as variation.

Phrase A could be performed first, repeated, followed by phrase B and then a return to phrase A, resulting in the tertiary form (AABA). Similarly, a rondo form could be used where the 'chorus' is given as a study phrase and a number of phrases A, B, C and D are created by various groups in the class. The dance form finally emerges as—chorus (everyone), phrase A (group A), chorus, phrase B (group B), chorus, phrase C (group

C), chorus, phrase D (group D), chorus. The teacher may well need to suggest the basis for each of the phrases, A, B, C and D. Third-year children seem to enjoy working in groups, particularly where the task given is different from that of other groups.

Suggestions have so far been concerned with the structure of the actual study and reasons for teaching studies have been given. The teaching of them can, however, present difficulties if the dance study is to lead on into more creative and individual work. A dance idea will, therefore, be taken as an example and worked out to show possible teaching methods.

One dance idea is a poem by D H Lawrence called 'Bats', upon which a dance study primarily concerned with skills of composition will be based. Set motifs will be composed and presented to the class—motifs stimulated by the images created in one of the lines of the poem, for example:

'A twitch, a twitter, an elastic shudder in flight,
And serrated wings against the sky.'

Firstly, the teacher needs to analyse the line of poetry, or whatever stimulus she is using for her study movements, as one would for any dance lesson preparation. The aim of this study example is to create one or two motifs from which other motifs can be developed by the pupils. Variations can be composed and phrases built up involving new material not initially given by the teacher. It is hoped that the dance study will give the children further understanding in the creation of movement images from the stimulus selected by the teacher—which, in this example, is a piece of poetry—and from these images finally composing a dance on bats. The children will, therefore, need guidance from the teacher in creating dance motifs which are 'meaty' enough for variation and further development.

If one considers the line of poetry suggested above two possible motifs could arise; 'A twitch, a twitter' could stimulate motif A, and 'An elastic shudder in flight, and serrated wings against the sky', motif B. The rest of the verse 'Like a glove thrown . . .' could be used later by the class to compose their motifs which could be repeated, varied and developed into phrases.

By presenting the children with motifs A and B which they master, a foundation is laid from which the pupils can be encouraged to compose their own motif C, and become involved in more creative work. The safety of the teacher's given motifs tends to build confidence in the children's abilities to perform, and inhibitions to dance can often be overcome allowing individual ideas to emerge in a dance form. Each child will have the same two motifs to refer back to, a security and conformity which third years enjoy.

If the teacher can discuss a little of her way of arriving at the given motifs from the stimulus, the children receive an insight into another person's approach to composing motifs and to the working of a dance idea through the analysis to the selection of movement ideas.

The study may be based on particular aspects of movement and/or composition, which it is hoped the children will come to understand in such a way as to facilitate transfer of learning into new and more creative situations. For example, if the aim of the study is concerned with the mastery and understanding of dance compositional facets of 'body rotations', the children will be more successful in gaining such understanding if the movement technique is 'clothed' in a dance idea rather than taught baldly as a sequence of actions. By presenting a dance idea involving in its analysis qualitative rotating situations ('Moon Dance') the children are more likely to be stimulated to dance the study— rather than move through the actions—and to understand the possible artistic expressions inherent in the dance movements.

Dance ideas	Analysis	Movement ideas
A verse from the poem *'Bats' by D H Law-* *rence* 'A twitch, a twitter, an elastic shudder in flight, And serrated wings against the sky, like a glove thrown up at the light And falling back.' solo	Sharp, darting gestures, angular, contrasted with a tense stretching, sud- denly releasing, back to a trembling. Frag- mented movements crossing one another, zig-zag, being thrown up, and dropping	Main stress: quality/space —bound-flow quality within a flickering move- ment and a firm stretching of the body suddenly released into a series of sudden movements. Such qualities are shaped within angles where joints and bony parts of the body become prominent and are contrasted with free- flowing rising and falling movements

Development of dance idea and teaching hints

Discussion
Very briefly explain to the children that the two motifs stimulated by the poem are given to show emphasis upon the qualities
and spatial aspects of movement. The children are to master these
motifs and use them in a dance stimulated by the verse of poetry.
Read the verse to them.

Work with movement ideas suggested by analysis
1 Introduce motif A by performing the motif for children to
observe and then to copy. Draw their attention to the kind of
bodily actions being used (a gesture, a turn or a jump) and the
parts of the body moving (shoulders or head twisting, right leg
gesturing, and so on).
> Actions of the body such as jumps, twists, gestures are prob-
> ably easier to observe and copy first and certainly essential
> for quality work later. The bodily actions represent a basic
> vocabulary upon which qualities and shapes are built and,
> therefore, are mastered first.

2 Observe and help children to master bodily actions by performing with them, describing the movements and correcting any
inaccuracies arising—individually, or as a group, whilst the children are moving.
> It is suggested that if the action is on one side of the body,
> repeat it on the other so that children do not become one-
> sided in mastering the motif.

3 Repeat the motif a few times and introduce any variations on
the 'twitch' and 'twitter'. For example, leg gestures could rise
higher or change direction, or begin close to the body and extend
further away in a series of 'twitch' and 'twitter' movements.
> Encouraging improvisation on the given motif is in order
> to equip children with a greater understanding of the com-
> positional possibilities within the motif, which later can be
> of value in their own dances.

4 The qualities used in the motifs could be introduced in much
the same way as the bodily actions have been—by observing and
doing. Twitching and twittering involves a bound-flow quality

within a flickering action which may be maintained in only one part of the body, the rest held alert.

Probably it will be necessary to extract the flickering action and teach its mastery involving the whole body in contrast with various isolated parts. Maybe phrases could evolve where a flickering action begins in a foot and spreads to incorporate the whole body.

The effort action of flickering could be tried with differing body actions, such as flickering gestures, or flicking turns. By experimenting beyond the context of the study, one is broadening the skill and understanding of the class with regard to the principles to be learnt in the study. One is also developing a broader range of movement upon which to draw in future creative situations.

5   The actual motif in its entirety could be performed by the whole group or in smaller groups incorporating some of the variations earlier worked upon. Shapes, qualities, floor and air patterns, and rhythms of the actions should begin to emerge with clarity and accuracy.

6   Motif B (suggested above) can similarly be introduced starting with a bodily aspect. For example, body design, working upon the parts of the body moving and the relationship of body part to body part, then concentrating on the spatial aspects and directions in space where the body is moving.

Constant correction of individuals and whole groups is necessary, using a combination of verbal instruction and practical demonstration. It is also very important to praise and encourage individual and group effort if improvement and perseverance is to occur.

7   Whilst working on the study movements it would also help the class if the teacher drew attention to the links between images in the verse of poetry and dance symbols in the study.

It may help children to understand a little of the process of abstraction and transformation, using the imagination in dance, if the teacher can explain how she used the poetic images to stimulate and create dance motifs.

8   The children could be encouraged to find their own methods of working, along similar guide-lines, to produce improvisations for the selection of a motif C stimulated by the line of poetry 'Like a glove thrown up'.

By this stage it is hoped inhibitions will have been over-come in the mastery of the study during which the class's attention tends to be fixed, for a large part of the time, upon the teacher moving, and all their effort centred upon mastering the various techniques.

Composition

The children should have three motifs with which to work—two given by the teacher and a third composed by the children.

1 Introduce variations on motifs A, B and C, such as changing the level in which the original movements of the motif were per-formed, or changing the qualities within the motifs, perhaps to achieve an acceleration in time, A different part of the body could be used from that of the original motif; for example, motif C which may well appear as a throwing action could be per-formed in a variation by a different part of the body.

Should the group be floundering, the teacher needs to suggest one or two variations for the class to perform to-gether and repeat after the original motifs.

2 Encourage repetition of perhaps a phrase they may have formed incorporating motif A repeated and followed by a varia-tion.

Repetition is vital if material is to be varied and developed.

3 As the class repeats the phrase of movement, suggest that this time after the variation they just keep moving to see what could follow.

It does not matter how small the movement is as long as the class move on from the phrase just completed to another variation or even a development section resulting from the phrase danced previously.

Some children, however, will not be able to continue beyond the repeated phrase and it is important for the teacher not to force them into moving. Nothing will be gained but greater selfconsciousness.

4 If any potentially new variations or developments have occurred, however unformed, encourage the children to repeat these phrases of movement to clarify and consolidate their ideas.

The teacher may find it necessary to point out the achieve-ments of the children in describing the new phrases they have created in terms of relationships with previous motifs:

is it another variation or has a tiny part of a previous
motif been used to develop into a contrasting phrase? Further understanding of the choreographic skills involved will
be encouraged by this kind of help from the teacher.

5   Work with motifs B and C can follow similarly until a number of phrases have been produced by the class incorporating the
material in motifs A, B and C.

The teacher needs to encourage the children to be independent in their work and not to rely on suggestions the
teacher could give.

6   Suggest that phrases be organised into a satisfying whole.

The teacher needs to point out that by performing one
phrase next to another, a certain relationship is created
between the phrases. There may be a strong or a slight
contrast produced. A speeding up of a climax could be
created, or tensions built up in one phrase and resolved in
the next.

Here the teacher's role is seen to be one of questioner and
clarifier of intentions, but it must not be laboured. Children
do need a period of undisturbed work in order to solve in
their own way individual problems of composition.

7   Suggest to the class that the dance has a beginning, then
grows, varies, develops and finally concludes, and that the movement begins and ends in stillness having travelled somewhere in
the space of the room.

The overall form of the dance should feel complete and
satisfying, as a unity, for each child.

The children will need help in recognising incomplete development of dance material and unnecessary or irrelevant
movements attached at the end of a completed dance form.
At this stage, children tend to keep moving even though the
most logical end of the dance may have been a previous
phrase of movement.

8   Finally, give opportunities for the finished compositions to be
danced through a number of times.

By dancing through their composition a few times the children can experience how their own dance feels as a whole
—how the climaxes, hesitations, tensions, resolutions, and
rhythms balance against each other and how the composition hangs together as a work of art, however modest.

The study of set movements must lead to creative work in later lessons. Further work on poems as dance ideas would be profitable, as would taking the poem 'Bats' in its entirety as a stimulus for a dance which does not involve study presentation of material. This example of a dance study may not be what many teachers regard as a study. Perhaps group dances (even if unfinished) pre-choreographed by the teacher are recognised more readily as a dance study. However, in the definition given earlier it is considered that any part of a dance composition imposed upon a class, whether it be a phrase, three motifs or more, is considered to be study presentation. The number of given movements depends very much upon the aim of the study. In the example above it was seen to be necessary to give two or three motifs for the children to manipulate and come to understand more fully the process of composition. There must be a stage later where the children compose their own motifs which are 'meaty' enough to vary, develop and extend into a dance form. Selection of the dance motif is a crucial part of composing as the motif is the seed from which the dance composition grows.

Observations of dance films and performances by professional dance companies will enhance the children's knowledge of dance composition and aesthetic appreciation of dance as an art form.

Dance subject   Violence

	Dance ideas	Analysis	Movement ideas
1	*Antagonism* duo	An action–reaction situation with attack defense and clashes. Tensions built up and resolved	Main stress: relationship. In opposition both in quality, eg fine-touch and strength and bodily, eg leg gesture answered by a toss of a head
2	*A violent creature* trio music: 'Rite of	Writhing distorted serpent-like form, menacing with a latent violence taking a bulk-like shape	Main stress: body. Strong twisting with held positions, one part of the body pulling against another. Vibrating as

Violence—*cont.*

	Spring'— Stravinsky (choose a short violent part) (background)		strength increases and group draws together then a bursting apart, body spreading and group spreading
3	*Gang warfare* group music: 'West Side Story' The Rumble— Bernstein (close relation- ship)	Vigorous action, attack- ing defending and recoiling movements. Whip-like action answered by a similar attack or a cowering retreat. Energetic leaps and lunges contrasted with wavering and weighing up, hovering before the attack (sus- pense building)	Main stress: quality. Thrusting, screwing (wringing) pressing effort actions in the attack involving leaping, con- trasted with moments of stillness and light sustained gestures body cowering, defending; could involve slashing turns and spin- ning to the ground in a gathering movement

Development of dance idea no. 1 with teaching hints

Discussion of dance idea

The dance subject 'Violence' should be discussed. The dictionary defines the quality of being violent as 'marked by great physical force, intimidating'. Other words, such as 'intense, vehement, passionate, furious [and] impetuous', are used in the definition. The class should discuss their own feelings about violence and then be encouraged to define 'antagonism' (definition 'active opposition'). Therefore, the dance will be on an 'action-reaction' situation.

Work with movement ideas suggested by analysis

1 Ask the class to react to either an action made by the teacher or a sound, for instance:

(a) A 'go-away' arm gesture—to send them from the discussion—then bring them back again with a 'beckoning' arm gesture.

(b) Add quality to the sound or gesture so that they go either quickly, slowly, firmly or with a feeling of fine-touch.

(c) During one of the 'go-away' travellings suddenly make a

loud noise (a drum, hand clap, bang on the floor) wait for their reaction.

(d) Continue the reactions to loud sudden sounds but ask the class for a specific action—a jump, a twist, rising, and sinking.

There is no necessity to take long over this part of the lesson but the class must understand that they are reacting to a given action or sound. Keep each phrase short and separate from the next.

2 Now explain briefly that you would like them to react in an opposite way to the teacher's actions and sounds. Examples:

(a) Beckon to them and they should retreat.

(b) Gesture them away and they should approach.

(c) A light rising gesture and they should reply with a strong sinking.

(d) A strong sinking gesture and the class replies with a light rising.

3 The class should now feel a fine-touch smooth gesture with one arm as the pupils do the opposite (firm, jerky) gesture with their other arm. See if they are able to feel the different tensions in each separate side of their body.

Change sides and give them time to assimilate the awkward feeling.

4 Rising with a fine-touch feeling in the top half of the body and then sinking with a feeling of firm tension in the lower half of the body. Then the opposite sensation, rising with firmness in the top half of the body sinking with a light sensation in the lower half of the body.

Try rising with the top half of the body whilst the bottom half is sinking.

They should feel the pull of opposing tensions for themselves in these exercises.

5 More subtlety should be introduced, still with two different parts of the body stressed in opposing gestures but not directly opposite. Examples:

As a shoulder encircles slowly, a knee may have a sudden short in-turning then out-turning gesture. Leave them to improvise with this idea.

They need to feel sure of what they are doing and may need help with ideas—suggest differences in time, direction, and weight.

Composition

1   Give the class the opportunity to discuss with a partner how to use the previous material to compose a duo. Remind them of the dance idea 'Antagonism' and of the previous discussion. The tensions experienced in their bodies in the first part of the lesson should be utilised in their compositions. Each may develop their own motifs in which are counter-tensions as in *5* above; or one of the pair might take a dominating role, therefore, her motifs will be powerful and her relationship clearly in control of the other more submissive partner. The counter-tension is then between the two and their motifs may be clearly contrasted. For example, a firm rising followed by an advancing with powerful arm gestures, contrasted with a more submissive motif involving turning, a curved body shape and a curved pathway.

2   They may wish to actually dance a 'combat' using the 'question and answer' form. The first dancer makes her movement statement and the second dancer replies with an opposing statement, and so on, until one dancer becomes dominant to resolve the situation. For example, the first dancer may start with an advancing motif and her partner reply, also advancing towards her and with rising; the first may then take her advancing motif past her partner who replies by repeating her advancing and rising again and again, building it into a powerful rhythmical phrase.

3   The relationship is one *versus* one, but it can be varied; one dancer may influence the other, or together they may be antagonistic to another imaginary force outside them both.

4   The climax of their dance should be clear and their conclusion definite. The antagonism may lead to violence or perhaps release into harmony. However, the main part of their composition is concerned with antagonism and there will be an element of attack, defence and clashing resulting from the dance idea.

Dance subject   'Primitive style'

	Dance ideas	Analysis	Movement ideas
1	*Moon Dance*	Circular shapes waxing and waning.	Main stress: space/quality. Body forms ball and
	group: 4*	Two crescent shapes	crescent shapes on the spot

'Primitive style'—*cont.*

	musical accompaniment: primitive drumming (close relationship)	emerging as one full circle. Mystical eerie quality a creeping which rises majestically to dominate the shy—a link with growth and maturity in man	or in stepping. Circle shape dominates group formations. Circles grow and shrink in size with sudden and sustained qualities. Body shapes can contract and extend. Rising and sinking movements involving changes of front; incorporating gliding and floating actions
2	*Animal Dance* solo Musical accompaniment: drumming (close relationship)	Animals in motion, in search for food, attacking in flight or in water Footprints, pecking and darting actions, on the alert. A swish of a tail a butt of ones horns contrasted with lolloping swooping or hovering	Main stress: body/quality. Quality of movement combined with particular movements of parts of the body in relation to the whole body can be observed in the animal and transferred into movement ideas. Dab-like movements of the head or flicking one of the hips—step patterns, gestures of arms and hands body spread or cowering or squatting are possibilities, together with interchanges of qualities of time and and weight factors
3	*Mask Dance* solo or groups, 3, 4 or 5 Musical accompaniment: drumming (close relationship)	Loss of one's own shape important. Face considered the seat of ones spirit. To wear another face one gives up one's own identity and takes on that of the mask. Movements become those of the mask's identity. Masks may be of animal heads or dream faces—fantastic or grotesque, distorted or of demons and devils. All very colourful and	Main stress: quality. Likely to lead to dramatic dances. If mask that of an animal head the dance idea no. 2 movement ideas would apply here when taking on the qualities and shape in the body and movement of the body of the animal in the mask. A mask created by each individual from their own fantasy needs to create an atmosphere, eg devil–fear–firm ponderous move-

'Primitive style'—*cont.*

| may have swinging bits attached | ments; screwing into the floor and thrusting away contrasted with spikey dab like movements or flicking actions |

* 4 is a significant number in primitive dances because of the moon's effect on the 4 seasons

Development of dance idea with teaching hints

Discussion of dance idea
This could involve the ritual significance of some of the ideas in the Moon Dance, such as travelling clockwise or to and fro with the movements facing the east. The circle shape is obvious in its link with the moon. The choice of four in a group is because of the moon's effects on the seasons. In primitive moon dances many of these motifs can be seen together with limping movements symbolising 'to be weak' and 'to begin a new moon'. The beginning is without power, like the new moon which finally overcomes the old dark moon. As a full moon it rises with majesty to dominate the sky.

Work with movement ideas suggested by analysis
1   Introduce travelling in circular floor patterns on first small then large circles, encouraging the body to lean into the centre of the circle and the arms to follow naturally. Also encourage a dropping into the circle and a rising out of it so that a lilting rhythm results.

The right side of the body can lean, followed by the left.

The natural rhythm of the circle shape is beginning to emerge with an accent on acceleration in speed halfway round the circle.

2   Encourage the large circles to be sustained and flowing and the small ones to gather speed into spinning.

The body will naturally want to open and scatter into a circling on the large circles and close and gather in the spinning.

Steps will be larger in the large circles and very small in the spinning.

3 As the body is scattering and dipping into large circles encourage the arms to gesture in curves, either leading with the right side (so travelling clockwise) or the left (travelling anticlockwise). If the right side scatters, the left will complete the movement by gathering in to close the body. The left side could then lead a high scattering movement completed by the right side in the same way. Sometimes a high scattering could be held with the body open and looking upwards and spinning around.

> This is one possible way of symbolising the shape of the moon in its course.

> Encourage phrase building by using voice or percussion, such as tambourine shaking or drumming (live or on record) as the class dance.

4 Play with the gathering/scattering movements to build phrases where one becomes the recovery for the other. Introduce jumping within the movement.

> Keep a free-flow, fine-touch quality throughout to facilitate the body movements.

5 As a contrast, the idea of a weak moon rising up to dominate the sky could be introduced by beginning close to the ground and creeping or limping (or any other form of travel symbolising weakness in the same sense). Gradually the movement rises increasing in tension to firm, powerful, dominant movements, which spread in the body from the centre, and gestures of arms and legs in the high level. A high position could be held from which the body lightly sinks, maybe to a crescent shape near or on the ground.

> There is an interplay of firmness with fine touch in which the natural areas for achieving the qualities, firmness low to the ground and fine touch in a higher level, are reversed[2].

6 Another suggestion could be that the full moon and crescent shapes are symbolised in body shapes which grow and shrink, extend from the centre and contract towards it again. The children could begin by lying on the floor in a crescent shape which arches and bends to re-form in a kneeling situation. From here the crescents are formed and disposed into different directions, finally bringing the children to their feet and involving the body in forwards, backwards or sideways arching and bending.

> Encourage moments of sudden quality within a fine-touch quality.

7   Suggest that at some point the crescent shape is held still in
the body and each child steps with a gliding quality to meet a
partner thus joining two crescent shapes to form a full circle,
symbolising a full moon.

8   One couple could now work with another couple to form
groups of four using the circle formation in the group. Some ideas
follow:

> Improvisation work on travelling on a circle, forming and
> reforming facing different directions, then all travel to the
> east of the room within rising and sinking actions. Rhyth-
> mic patterns will emerge within the movements and spatial
> forms, such as rising and sinking in common, one sustained,
> the others suddenly shooting upwards; or a very sustained
> rising motif in unison where arm gestures and a leg gesture
> could rise up to the highest point, making contact with the
> next person to form a circle. The circle could grow and
> shrink in size, the dancers keeping contact or not but em-
> phasising the proximity as the circle contracts and the dis-
> posal as the circle expands. This could be danced with a
> gliding quality which increases in tension and speed to
> vibrant trembling and confusion shown in group form and
> body shape.
>
> Drumming accompaniment could be played at this point
> to add a rhythmic framework.
>
> These are only some of the ideas that the group could
> achieve based on the dance idea. The children's imagina-
> tions will be fired if the significance of the dance symbols
> is stated and references to the primitive lunar dances made,
> for such information clarifies the heritage of Dance today.

Composition

1   From all the previous improvisations the group may select
any of the movements that resulted from groups or individual
work. For example, the group could begin with the idea of the
rising of the creeping new moon which reaches dominance and
power and finally sinks to nothing. This section could contrast with
a flowing section of curving gathering and scattering movements.

> Accompaniment could be used here.

2   Guidance needs to be given to develop an awareness on the
part of the children of the emerging form of the dance and to vary

and develop material from selected motifs (building repeats into phrases). The aim is not to string together little phrases, but to vary or develop the dance material in one phrase to produce another similar or contrasting phrase. Each phrase should grow out of the previous phrases, creating tensions or resolving them, creating contrasts or similarities, and so on.

As the children work, the teacher needs to describe the relationships created between one phrase and the next, in order to develop an awareness in the children of the varied relationships that can occur during the juxtaposing of their dance phrases. This process of organising dance phrases must continue until the children have achieved a dance that satisfies their intentions.

3 Situations can evolve in fours which do not appear in other numbers. Four is an even number, a stable number. It may divide into pairs but it still remains stable until one and three occur. Then the instability appears, the conflict and the drama. Often the group formation can become square and set and sometimes difficult to break. The tendency for pairs to result may make the reforming of the group more difficult as the couples begin to work out different dances.

These are moments when the teacher can help as she sees them occur. She needs to ask the group's intentions and question their relevance to the dance idea. The children must be encouraged to abandon any irrelevant or extraneous movement.

4 Suggest shortness of the dance to encourage simplicity of form and a paring down of the basic motifs. Only the vital movements need be present, so that the import of the dance remains uncluttered, strong and clear.

When one has developed a small vocabulary of movements (as these children should have done) it is easy for favourite movements to appear in every dance, whether they satisfy the dance idea or not. The teacher needs to draw the children's attention to this and help them to find new movements from new situations presented to them.

Dance subject   'Pop star'

	Dance ideas	Analysis	Movement ideas
I	*Worship of a Pop Star* group music: 'Walk on the Wild Side' by Bernstein, or a 'pop' record (background)	Dreaming, drifting hypnotic growing excitement followed by hysterical reaction and grasping	Main stress: quality. Floating gestures and steps, rolling of head contrasted with vibrating and shaking extending away from the body, sustained firm gathering gestures
2	*Instrumentalists* group music: a pop record with clear instrumentation eg 'Abraxas' by Santana (background)	Guitars—swaying of body with strumming hand movements. Drums—vigorous waving of arms into strong hitting actions. Vocalist—strong pulsating throughout the body contrasted with sharp held positions	Main stress: body gestures. Shoulder and trunk twisting with rhythmical stepping patterns. Drums—rhythmical thrusting of head and arms into different directions with very clear accents. Vocalist—centre and hips initiate energetic successive movements throughout the body, head particularly important
3	*Rise and fall of a Pop Star* solo music: eg 'Time' from 'Dark Side of the Moon' by Pink Floyd (background)	Gradual build up of image and importance as an overpowering figure emerges with a dominating presence inevitably followed by a decline	Main stress: body/quality. Movements increase in size quality of firmness increases to powerful rhythmical climax, arms gesturing away from body, hips very mobile and head tossed from side-to-side. The decline may be sudden or gradual as movements decrease in size and firmness leave the body which ends quite limp

Development of dance idea no. 1 with teaching hints

Discussion of dance idea

Discuss the children's reactions when listening to their favourite Pop Star, how they might react at a 'live' concert and what they have seen of other people's behaviour. Explain that you wish to translate these reactions into suitable movements for a dance. Whatever music is chosen will, of course, influence the dance and as they listen indicate how it is possible to use the music to set the mood (with it staying in the background rather than becoming all-important).

Work with movement ideas suggested by analysis

1 Commence sitting in a dancing position (both legs to one side) and put on the background music. Slowly circle the head, until it drops to the chest and then circles round up and back ready to drop down again.

> Keep this movement very smooth to help produce an hypnotic feeling.

2 Gradually develop the circling, spreading it through the body. Include the top half of the body (still in the sitting position) then move into kneeling (still circling with the head and top half of body), eventually rising onto the feet and taking the circling into a circling floor pattern.

> By rising onto the knees and then stepping up first with one foot then another, the movement can be kept continuous and remain smooth. The class may be feeling slightly dizzy by now.

3 Gradually the circling phrase can come to an end, the circles getting smaller, finally to a stillness. Hold the stillness for a time.

> The dizzy sensation at the end of the circling phrase should link up with the discussion about reactions at pop concerts.

4 The next phrase starts with shaking and vibrating, first in the head and then in the arms. They start close to the body, shaking out and away from the body and suddenly returning to the body ready to repeat the vibrating motif again in a different direction. This continues building up to a frenzy and ends in a sudden stop with a held extended position. The vibrating motif has built to a phrase.

The class can be 'talked through' the circling phrase and then the vibrating phrase. The transition is simple and it is not necessary to break the mood of the dance in order to explain the next movement. Music will be played in the background but not too loudly as the class need to hear the teacher.

5   From the end of the vibrating phrase (sudden stop in extended position) fingers curl and grasp, followed by wrists and arms, then the top of the body curls over into a grasping dragging downwards, slowly sinking—this is quite strong, there is a release of tension and a lifting of the body, then the curling, grasping starts again.

Repetition of a phrase can build up involving grasping and releasing, a sinking then rising with differences in tension using different directions in space.

6   Leave the class to improvise their phrases having discussed how they relate to the dance idea; for instance the circling phrase is repetitive like the beat of the music and rather hypnotic, as is some 'pop' music. The vibrating phrase builds to a frenzy of movement like hysteria at some pop concerts. The grasping, dragging phrase is linked with fans trying to touch their idols and perhaps tearing at their clothes.

Encourage them to add their own ideas during the improvisation. Keep music playing in the background.

Composition

1   Divide class into groups keeping the numbers odd to prevent the development of pairs. They should discuss the dance idea together and may as a group:

(a) Show within the group their different reactions to a pop star, or

(b) All react in the same way, or

(c) One or more of the group could dance 'the pop star' and the remainder react to him/them.

2   They should use the previous phrases as a basis of composition. Rather than being satisfied with a sketchy outline they can vary and develop the phrases to structure the dance.

(a) The circling phrase (in 2 above) may be used as a group motif, the whole group starting in a small circle and gradually dispersing as the phrase increases in size; or, each individual, brought into a group circling pathway going into and away from a common focus point as the phrase increases in size. Perhaps a more interesting way of using the phrase might be if each member of the group started the phrase at a different time, or part way through the phrase, so that it is danced at a different stage— some in the circular pathway going close to the ground with head-circling as they pass others at an earlier stage of the phrase.

(b) The vibrating phrase (in 3 above) could gradually spread through the group, the climax in the phrase being shared by the whole group. Again there may be a common direction— the whole group keeping together as directions change—or each dancer moving in different directions. Different levels can be used creating a more interesting grouping; some vibrating high, others at a medium level and remainder low. The sudden movement back into the body could be used to spark off other people in a group to start the phrase so that all are not dancing at the same time.

(c) The grasping phrase (number 5 above) could be used by the group in a way similar to the other two phrases, or the group as a whole could travel in a circular pathway engulfing other areas of the room. The group must start close together, slowly expanding in shape and all the children travelling to encircle another place then closing in together again.

3   Discuss their compositions with the individual groups rather than the class as a whole, thus keeping their individuality.

It is necessary to encourage groups individually, suggesting different ideas to the group should they be having difficulty; for example, the pop star who has to escape from his fans ends exhausted—in a trance—or a frenzy. Probably the music will influence their ideas.

4   Discuss the music with the class. They may wish to use another piece or each group use a different piece (this is more difficult to organise) as it is purely background music to set the mood of the dance. For part of the time groups could practise without their music. It is essential the music does not hinder composition and the class should be made aware of this problem in order to prevent reversion to 'pop dancing' without any form.

5   As dances are completed—and this will probably take more than one or two lessons—give the class the opportunity to watch

each other's dances, and discuss them, developing their powers of observation and evaluation. Keep discussion constructive and guide their observations, for example, 'look for clear phrasing and motifs'. This age group can be tactless and unkind without thinking. Ask what they liked about the compositions and why.

It is up to each teacher to assess her class deciding whether they are able to perform in individual groups or would be happier dancing alongside other groups. Half the class dancing at a time might solve this problem.

Dance subject 'Zorba's Dance' — music from the film 'Zorba the Greek'

(Suitable for beginners)

	Dance ideas	Analysis	Movement ideas
1	*Music stimulating dance study* solo into group	Changing from a deliberate ponderous beginning to exhileration and sheer excitement	Main stress: body. Impulsive movements spreading and contracting from the centre, then legs in stepping patterns and gestures
2	*Release* solo (close relationship)	A reluctance a withdrawal which ventures outwards gradually surging into a release of energy	Main stress: quality. Bound flow with small gestures, gradual build up to larger gestures and a much freer use of space and an increase in speed
3	*Greek 'National type' steps* (linear form) group (close relationship)	Calm beginning building up to exciting rhythmic patterns and very energetic leg movements. Upright carriage of the body as the group travels sideways in a linear formation	Main stress: body. Leg gestures very important leading into steps which travel sideways. Rhythms are very prominent. Top of body held upright with arms outstretched

Development of dance idea no. 1 with teaching hints

Discussion of dance idea

Listen to the music and discuss the simplicity of the phrasing and the clear structure of the music—how it builds up gradually in speed affecting the mood of the music. Explain that as it is a dance study all will work together on the same movements.

> The phrasing is so simple that even after their first hearing it should be possible to go straight into the first phrase.

Work with movement ideas suggested by analysis

1 Start from a comfortable sitting position for a dance, that is both legs to one side with knees bent, and ask the class to:

(a) Push their 'centre' forwards—that is the area around their waistline. This causes the top half of their body to spread their backs to arch and their heads to tilt backwards; then

(b) Ask the class to gradually change the situation and to suck their 'centre' in, causing the top half of their body to close, their backs round over and their heads sink down.

> Work on this until there is a good response as sensitivity in the 'centre' of the body is vital to the individual child's command of their own body as an instrument for dance.

2 Fit the above simple phrase into the ebb and flow of the first few bars of the music, starting the phrase small, gradually increasing in size and gradually standing; end with a slow, spreading turning around back to facing front (phrase A).

> It is necessary for the teacher to have worked on this study, so that she knows exactly how she wants the phrases to be danced and would be able to demonstrate accurately to the class when necessary.

3 The next phrase is very similar to the first as is the musical phrase:

(a) Use the 'side centre' of the body to spread the side of the body causing one arm to gradually rise and the body to stretch and open on one side; then

(b) As in the first phrase, the opposite happens; the 'side centre' sucks the side back in, 'closing' that side.

(c) This can then be developed by stepping to the side on the 'opening', retreating back a little on the 'closing'—start the movement small and gradually increase the size ending once again with a slow, spreading turn.

(d) The phrase is repeated on the other side, these two together form one longer phrase (phrase B).

> We must stress that the teacher should have felt these movements for herself. What we have described is necessarily very simple indeed because of the difficulty of communicating more complicated movements in written word, but we would suggest the teacher uses these as 'basic steps' for her study and develop them to her own requirements.

4   The music changes, slowly at first but insistently to a very lively bouncy rhythm. A 'Greek-type' (folk) stepping pattern, starting slowly and gradually increasing in speed, fits the rhythm and the style of the music and travels around the room (phrase C); that is, body upright, arms outstretched, facing front to start but facing sideways during the stepping; right foot step to the side, left foot step across right foot, then both feet come together with a slight jump as the body turns to the left, another small jump as the body turns back to the right (in preparation for the first step to the right starting again) this is repeated and the speed is gradually increased.

> Again we stress that this is a simple basis and it is necessary for the teacher to work on it and to find where she wants the accents, perhaps some leg gestures or nods of head. She will know how her class would respond whether she can add gestures and still keep to a stepping pattern.

5   Link the phrases A, B and C together to the music and the study will end when the travelling is in full swing.

> Work on this until all in the class are clear and know exactly how to go from one phrase to the next—that is, clear transitions—each phrase linking naturally with the next; in this case phrase B is a natural development from phrase A and phrase C is a development of phrase B.

6   Add a simple relationship to the study, appoint certain individuals to start the stepping pattern; the others remain still until they are approached by one of the appointed 'leaders' then they take hands and join in the stepping pattern. Gradually a number of lines of dancers will be travelling around the room performing together.

This is also a useful way to teach the step, encouraging the the class to help each other.

7 This has formed the class into groups and now is the time for further discussion. Ask the class to find their own ways of finishing the dance study within their own group. Listen to the music —they may wish to finish their dance before the end as it goes on for some time after the initial phrases.

Composition

1 The first part of their composition has been set as a study; when selecting material for their own part of the composition, they may wish to repeat, develop or vary the phrases they have been given. The study should have taught them more than a body technique, they should have discovered something about the structuring of a dance, however simple—for example, that it can start small, gradually increase in size and then travel.

Discuss with the class how this simple structure could be developed within a group, perhaps how a small phrase can grow and pass through a group to increase the size of the phrase and the number of people dancing the phrase.

2 They may wish to introduce new ideas to end their dance, more 'national-type' steps would link up with the last phrase of the study. Examples:

(a) Lively spinning on the spot with hands clapping and feet stamping.

(b) Group circling holding hands, first in one direction, stamping to change direction.

(c) Holding a partner spinning around with different speeds, different holds, changing partners.

These are suggestions for the class to discuss, many of the groups will have their own ideas which are entirely different and, of course, this should be encouraged.

3 Draw attention to the group shapes which emerged during the study, such as a group travelling in a line. Discuss other possibilities—circle, partners within a group, angular group shapes, curved group shapes.

By observing the group dances at the end they can discover more about group shapes. To develop this further each group could teach its ending to the study to the whole class. This means that the class is dancing as a whole group;

large group dances should be fun and fleeting at this stage as there is little to be gained in spending hours of practice simply to produce a class dance. This age group will benefit much more by being given the opportunity to discover their own compositional ideas.

Chapter 5

Dance Ideas for 14-15 year Age Group

During the fourth year an adolescent needs to conform and a more sophisticated, mature behaviour develops more strongly. Acceptable dance ideas for this age group should be identifiable with the children's own peer group interests. An example of this is the dance subject 'Clothes'.

The teacher often finds that children who in the previous year became inhibited during creative work now enjoy a more creative approach to their dance lessons. But there is also often the reverse where children who enjoyed creative work in the previous year are now developing an awkwardness and selfconsciousness. Opportunities for both creative work and study presentation should therefore be given by the teacher. The mastery of bodily skills, particularly those given in study form, tend perhaps to be valued and enjoyed amongst the pupils, rather more than originality of movement ideas—the fourth year often being an age of 'creative decline'.

Personal preferences amongst the pupils for either spatial or effort dances are shown clearly at this stage, but it is important that dance ideas utilise all aspects of movement—spatial, rhythmic, quality and bodily facets—and relationships (both duo and group). The dance subject 'Clothes' incorporates spatial, body and quality aspects within the developed dance idea 'Hats', whereas the dance subject 'The Sea' has a quality stress.

More spatially stressed dance ideas are often enjoyed by the more intellectually able groups, who seem to be able to appreciate the degree of abstraction involved in the movement ideas, and can understand the spatial relationships inherent in the dance idea in such a way as to use these relationships in their compositions, and a 'harmony' in movement is greatly enjoyed. (For further reading in space harmony, see [2], [3].)

The less intellectual groups tend to enjoy and appreciate 'harmony' in movement at the practical level through a kinaesthetic awareness rather than at a level of intellectual appreciation.

The addition of 'props'—such as wearing clothing to influence the movement—can help the teacher tackle the problem of some pupil's reluctance to become involved in creative work. Being able to see, touch and wear a piece of clothing, and to dance in it, gives a first-hand experience of the particular dance idea. It also presents an opportunity for students to dress up—something we all enjoy doing. Wearing costume also adds another dimension to the movements produced, especially if the costume is a long, flowing skirt. Shapes, curves, folds can be created in the skirt which can swirl and enfold through the movements of the legs and hips beneath. These movements need to be exaggerated to become fully apparent in the movements of the skirt. What better way of developing awareness of leg movements with a group of adolescents who are selfconscious, yet very fashion conscious! Leg movements have to be clear—gestures occurring near to, around or away from the body if the skirt is to move with grace and flow.

Dance ideas for the fourth year should also cater for the experience of the sensation of action as well as the mastery of technique. Many children during this fourth year are maturing physically, becoming larger in build, heavier hipped and consequently do not enjoy exposing themselves to athletic feats. They do enjoy achieving the sensations of actions such as elevation which can be achieved by pupils who may not enjoy vigorous leaping. Dance studies could utilise this very point, as in dance study 'Sounds of Silence' where the sensations of rising and spreading are all important but do not actually lead to jumping.

Pupils begin to develop this ability to see the relationships between shapes, actions, rhythms and qualities of movements in their own compositions and can begin to appreciate them both kinaesthetically and intellectually.

Movement characteristics of fourth years
The development of body centre awareness in the third year is further increased in this year and a growing harmony in the flow of the movement from one part of the body to another continues—

perhaps due to a desire on the part of the children to improve general body poise, thereby acquiring elegance.

The children are capable of moving several parts of the body simultaneously. However, there is still a reluctance to use the legs for jumping and gesturing, as in the previous year. This could well be due to the physical maturing of the adolescent and a desire that they should not appear ungainly. Jumping is an activity in which the body needs to be thrust into the air by the hips, legs and feet, and when performed well can be accomplished by a sensation of suspended flight as the chest is lifted upwards. A certain degree of leg awareness is required, especially when the body is actually in the air and the legs are gesturing, as often they are. Quite a degree of mastery of the body is required to perform jumps with an apparent ease and with a sensation of flying. Fourth and third years often show great difficulty in mastering jumping. However, this does not mean that the activity itself should be avoided—rather it may be necessary to present jumping situations in study form. Jumping is a dimension in dance that is central to the activity of dancing. As Laban[2] himself stated '. . . Of all body functions the skips, leaps and jumps are the most characteristic dancing actions because they can constitute the main efforts of a whole dance.'

By the fourth year, repetition of given movements should be even more easily and accurately copied—particularly rhythmic stepping patterns. Such dance subjects as 'Popular dances of the past' foster and utilise this developed skill. In improvisory work, clarity in floor and air patterns can occur in some children's work.

The ability to shape effort actions is also developing during improvisations. The qualities of the movements can often be produced in most parts of the body, and the combination of shape and effort content is often achieved in their performances. Dance ideas stressing clarity of shapes in the air, and floor patterns, foster the development of skills to clarify the inherent shapes in the effort actions, for example, 'slashing' will make a rounded or twisted shape[3].

The fourth-year children often show interest and enjoyment in clarifying rhythmic phrases, and can become absorbed in work that involves an interplay of one rhythmic pattern with another in movement. An example is in a duo situation—each dancer with the same rhythmic phrase, where one begins the phrase and the other starts at different intervals of time, thereby creating varied rhythmic effects such as syncopation. Dance ideas need to present learning situations involving such work—see the dance ideas under dance subject 'Sounds of Silence'.

The children's own compositions should be dynamically alive. Climaxes involving increases of tension or speed should be understood by some and seen in their dances. Transitions from one effort to another can be facilitated by using strong contrasts, for example, thrusting into floating. More able classes will be able to master subtler changes such as floating to flicking or gliding[3].

Dance ideas should cater for a developing skill in orientating movements in space, see dance subject 'Growth'. Further clarity should develop in group formations and in air and floor patterns within the groups. The basic expressions of rising, sinking, advancing and retreating movements—and many others—are beginning to be more fully understood by this age group within the context of a dance. This new-found understanding needs developing further and the work involved in the dance subject 'Sounds of Silence' attempts to achieve this task.

Composition

There is a further stress on the completion of dances and the performing of completed dances, to improve the body skills within the dance, and to polish the overall performance of the dance.

Presentation of material needs a balance between setting learning situations from which improvisations occur, and teaching dance studies. The latter will help those who have lost their confidence in their own creative work. Some children who have overcome their inhibitions of previous years may want to work creatively.

Pupil's dances should be longer and more thoroughly thought out. Dances should reveal a basic skill in the process of variation within the composition. The degree of development of motifs will be limited. There should, however, appear further clarity in the formation of dance motifs and phrases.

Punctuation of phrases will be clearer and more refined, involving hesitations, suspended moments and pausing for various lengths of time.

Some children will begin to develop an understanding of dance form by analysing their own finished compositions, recognising motifs, repeats of motifs and phrases, variations, and development of new material.

Fourth years enjoy recognising some of the classical forms which may arise in their own dance compositions or dance studies presented by the teacher, for example, canon, binary, tertiary, rondo theme and variation. Some children find difficulty recognising and analysing dance forms intellectually, but may experience the satisfaction of achieving a completed dance form, and a kinaesthetic experience when the form is complete and when the end of their own composition is reached.

By the fourth year the pupils should have developed the ability to distinguish between dramatic and lyrical dance, and to create dances either lyrical or dramatic, thereby being able to create 'moods' in their dances through the medium of movement.

There is a tendency for solo work to be rejected and group work to become a very necessary part of a successful dance lesson. Again, a link with the physical and emotional inhibitions of the fourth-year child can be made. There is a retreat from situations which reveal one's ideas and, through one's ideas, oneself. The desire to conform within a group, to lose one's identity and to take on that of the group is more appealing. Group sensitivity can be further developed, the groups showing an ability to organise themselves as a functioning unit to a certain degree.

Groups of five continue, sometimes splitting into duo and trio, interweaving, forming circles contracting and extending away and towards the centre, or sinking. Two groups of five can cross in linear formation and merge or encircle one another without too much muddle. In groups of five the children can acquire the satisfaction of feeling part of a group—the odd number being a very workable unit.

Dance ideas should continue to encourage exploration of differing choreographic possibilities in duo, trio, groups of four and five, and in larger groups and should develop an understanding for the relevance of group formations with respect to the dance idea (see dance idea 'Mushrooms' from dance subject 'Growth').

Members of a group who find difficulty in voicing their ideas should be given opportunities and encouragement to become positively active in the group work, whilst those who tend to dominate and lead should be encouraged to follow and listen to others. All this can be helped by the choice of group formations, eg each taking a turn as leader in the linear group. Dance subjects, such as 'Growth', give such opportunities in their dance ideas by beginning with individual work and developing into duos, trios and then into larger groups. Here is given the experience of a contrast between the individual within a group and conformity in the group during unison movement.

Music

A wide range from 'pop' music to modern classical can be appreciated. It is advisable not to force classical or 'heavy popular' music upon fourth-year groups who may reject it, perhaps because of its unfamiliarity. There are many 'good' pieces of music in the 'pop' range suitable for stimulating or accompanying dance ideas. The folk song section often appeals because of its rendering of the soul, its immediate impact upon the listener, due perhaps to its simplicity of expresion in musical form. Dance ideas should try to include as wide a range of musical styles and types as possible so that the children are introduced to the many possibilities music has to offer the dancer.

Dance subject   Popular dances of the past

(Suitable for beginners)

	Dance ideas	Analysis	Movement ideas
1	*Charleston* group music: traditional jazz (close relationship)	Very lively Charleston steps, full of vitality, vibrating and brittle	Main stress: body/quality. Sudden gestures of arms and legs in the stepping; steps learned as a study but the energetic quality most important
2	*Waltz* group music: 'olde-tyme waltz' (any)	A lilting, flowing feeling of going on and on, light and relaxing; the waltz rhythm has a lifting and a dropping	Main stress: body/rhythm. Master basic waltz step then experiment with other waltz-type steps, eg with a hesitation, turns,

Popular dances of the past—*cont.*

	(close relation-ship)		leg gestures, rising and sinking
3	*Hand-jive* *solo* music: rock 'n' roll (any) (close relation-ship)	Isolated hand gestures, a routine to the basic rhythm of the music; gradually the hands lead the body into the areas of space which are hinted at in the routine, eg up-down, side-to side; the rhythm becomes less important	Main stress: body/space. A hand-waving routine which is repeated as it stands; gradually rest of body firstly leans in the directions indicated then goes further into that direction, eg an upwards, downwards hand-jive and the body rises and sinks. A side-to-side hand jive and the body travels first to one side then the other; the rhythm will be cut across and the final com-position could almost be a 'space study'

Development of dance idea no. 1 with teaching hints

Discussion of dance idea

This age group will be very interested to hear about the history of dance and how the Charleston was a sudden, dramatic change in popular dance as a reaction after the First World War. Clothes, and music were affected in what is now known as the 'Roaring Twenties'. Encourage them to do some research themselves and perhaps some written work on the subject. More mature groups might wish to link all these dance ideas together forming their own anthology, for example, the Charleston used in a dance idea—'The Aftermath of War'.

Work with movement ideas suggested by analysis

1 Teach the basic steps without music.
   (a) Start with toes turned in, feet slightly apart, and slowly spin on balls of feet until heels are close together, then spin back to original position. Repeat—build up the speed and keep the quality lively. As soon as this is mastered add hand

gestures—small circling movements in front of body within the same simple rhythm.

These steps are not very difficult; try to go quickly from one to the next. Whilst technique is important strive for a lively quality, but this will not be there if they find the actual steps laborious.

(b) Using the basic step (a), progress by transferring body weight onto one foot during the step and releasing the other to come slightly clear of floor during the stepping. Repeat with other foot.

Although this is a simple progression, girls have had difficulty with this step and find the following steps much easier.

(c) Still using the basic step (a) this time step forwards and then backwards. The released foot swings forward to gesture in front either onto the floor or with a kick; similarly there is a backwards gesture onto the floor (no kick). In this step the arms swing easily in opposition to the legs.

Having seen this step performed before they will probably have their own ideas on how it should be done.

(d) Stepping around on the spot using every beat to transfer from one foot to the other with just one swivel in each step (the heel first starting towards the body and ending facing out). Hands quiver high above the head or swing around a long rope of beads.

This is an even quicker step than the others and can be used as a 'link-up' between steps.

(e) Standing on the spot, a knee gesture, high, with the hands both coming down to slap it—four with one knee, four with the other—(facial gestures: ooo—ah!) add some authenticity and hilarity to this step).

It could be a measure of the confidence of the class if they were able to feel the quality these movements had, and still have.

(f) There is a more thrilling step—including sliding on one foot first to one side (on right foot sliding to the left) then to the other side (on left foot sliding to the right) followed by two slides to the left without transferring the weight and then two slides to the right without transferring the weight. It is necessary to start from a standing position then on one foot slide to the side without taking the weight off the floor. In this step the arms do exaggerated circular gestures in front of the body and in rhythm with the step.

This is fun to try, and ask them to practise at home.

2   Once something of the steps has been mastered ask them to dance them through to music, linking them up as they dance. If possible, try to start with something quite slow and gradually build up the speed.

This is not easy as most Charleston records are fast, but there are some a little slower. It may work if the record is played at a slower speed. Alternatively, provide a rhythm for them with a tambourine or by clapping.

Composition

1   Discuss the possibilities of linking these steps into a dance idea, for instance:

(i) 'Aftermath of War'—using the arm gestures as a basis for a sad, slow beginning, the encircling, *1* (a) might lift at the sides, come over the head and bow the head down, the forwards and backwards swing, *1* (c), reaching forwards hopefully and then sinking back—gradually during the dance the speed increases, the music's volume is increased, until the Charleston is being danced in a frenzy.

(ii) 'Fashion in the 20s'—use steps to show off fashion, kicking legs for short skirts, swinging long beads included in the motifs, hand gestures showing off 1920s.

(iii) 'How the Charleston was invented'—a slow build-up of the various steps, perhaps starting from a heel tapping to the rhythm of the music. One person could pass on a new idea—a hand gesture, perhaps, until all the group are discovering ideas for themselves.

Let each group decide on their idea. Pupils may wish to dance a straightforward Charleston, but, if in a group, they will need to work out a routine together. Point out to class it is not necessary for them all to be dancing the same steps at the same time.

2   The stylised arm gestures and leg gestures might be used as a framework for a composition, for instance:

(i) The encircling action, *1* (a), could start small and increase in size, gradually taking the body into turning or a circling pathway, first one side then the other to lead, which is how the arm gestures happen in the Charleston.

(ii) The swinging forwards and backwards of the arms, *1* (c), could grow through the body introducing a reaching forwards and a sinking backwards which might lead into rising and sinking.

3 The spatial patterns and pathways of the Charleston steps are very clear and the group might use these to influence composition, for instance:

Travel around each other with the 'swivel' step, *1* (d), or make pathways to cross each other's with the 'kicking' step, *1* (c) The 'sliding' step, 1 (f), would be suited to dancing side-by-side or facing a partner going in opposite directions.

4 There are many varieties of steps and combinations of steps which some girls may know already. Encourage inventiveness and help them not to be limited only to the steps given. There should be moments of stillness to add sharpness to the dance as the Charleston was in fact a very 'brittle' dance.

Dance subject   Music — 'Sounds of Silence' by Simon & Garfunkel

(Suitable for beginners)

	Dance ideas	Analysis	Movement ideas
1	*Dance study* solo into group music: close relationship	Lingering phrases in keeping with the quality of the music—people passing each other without actually meeting; motifs danced in isolation; drawing together of group as music progresses with a more energetic response building to a frenzied climax which dies away	Main stress: body/quality. A gradual build-up of a phrase starting from the centre and increasing in size keeping a feeling of sustainment; some sharp contrasts with more sudden direct movements, some 'primitive type', and ending again with the sustained motif
2	*Words of the song as the chief stimulus*	Rather profound ideas about loneliness; an attempt to communicate with others which	Main stress: quality/ relationship. Changing from bound to free flow; gestures extend

'Sounds of Silence' by Simon & Garfunkel—*cont.*

	solo	fails	away from body, counter tensions in the body explored
	music: close relationship		
3	*Space study*	A lonely group as each member is linked only by the movements, otherwise they do not relate to each other. They dance an identical study, but each person starts at a different part of the study, therefore ending at different times. No-one is dancing the same movement at the same time as any-one else, they are dancing in canon	Main stress: body/space. Clearly defined shapes, rising, sinking, using diagonal pathways across the body, advancing retreating, arms and leg gestures clearly defined but kept simple
	group		
	music: close relationship		

Development of dance idea no. 1 with teaching hints

Discussion of dance idea

Listen to the music, discuss loneliness and what the songwriter meant by phrases such as 'the sound of silence' or 'people talking without speaking'. Reference to the neon light flashing, which comes towards the end of the song is important as it symbolises a way of communicating today and some people feel an alienation to this type of communication. The class may wish to express their own ideas here and try to discover the songwriter's thoughts when he was composing. It is interesting to observe how the music relates to the words of the song, climaxes building together as in 'people vowed and prayed to the neon god they made' Another line of discussion might proceed from the idea of moving in a 'lonely' way, and its opposite, in an 'outgoing' way. This should lead straight into the beginning of the work with movement ideas.

Work with movement ideas suggested by analysis
1   Leading from the discussion ask class to go towards other

people in an outgoing way—eagerly, looking them in the eye, touching them, perhaps shaking hands.

This can be done without dancing, or may be danced in a specific way, for example, rushing directly forwards and stopping suddenly, then a short dance phrase made from the action of shaking hands, perhaps building up a very rhythmical—shake, stop, shake, stop, shake, shake, shake, stop.

2 Ask class to repeat the above phrase or phrases feeling themselves holding back reluctantly—see how this change of feeling will affect their movement. Exaggerate changes that occur and make clear what they are.

'Holding back' can best be felt in the centre of the body. The centre of the back can be pulling the rest of the body back even though the body may be travelling forwards. The quality felt should be one of being withdrawn, cautious, not wishing to communicate; this is known as 'bound-flow' quality; the opposite being gay, abandoned, carefree—'free-flow' (Laban).

3 Discuss how the class were able to feel the change from *1* to *2* and the importance of being aware of the 'centre' of the body. When the centre advances forwards there is a feeling of going easily (perhaps to meet someone), but when the centre pulls back and the travel is forwards there is a definite feeling of reluctance (not to meet).

This age group should be aware of their ability to express their emotions through the medium of dance.

4 Once the group has become aware of the possibilities discussed above, a dance study can be introduced which is performed with an emphasis on 'bound-flow'.

(a) First verse of the song.

(i) Starting position standing, a small 'hello' gesture using right hand involving a slow circling at waist level with the 'centre' of the body initiating the movement. Left hand repeats the circling.

(ii) Right hand circling again with a larger movement, causing body to rise and sink slightly; left hand again repeats; Thus, the phrase starts first on one side of body and repeats on the other side, and so on.

(iii) With both hands starting low from side of the body

make one big rising circle to high above the head; hands to come together to sink the body down low.

(iv) A reversal of this sinking with both hands together—the body rising upwards (hands leading) with an impulsive movement and slowing as hands reach high together then part to move down to the sides of the body in a sustained way.

This last motif (iv) mirrors the words 'the sound of silence' and is often repeated throughout the dance. The whole of the phrase should be felt as sustained with the top half of the body active all the time, leaning to the side, looking upwards, downwards, and so on.

(b) Second verse—referring to walking in dreams.

(i) From the position in which they stand ask the children to walk past each other without looking at them; changing directions unexpectedly and keeping on a medium level, the sudden change of direction breaking the more sustained walk.

(ii) The above phrase ends with a sudden sharp movement from the head, first in one direction then another direction followed by a slow sinking.

(iii) As 'the sound of silence' phrase is repeated at the end of verse so is the motif.

The group will now have moved together but there is a studied lack of contact with each other; they should, however, be aware of the pathway through the group and when this is repeated a group pattern should emerge; there should still be a feeling of holding back in the body.

(c) Third verse—referring to ten thousand people talking without speaking and hearing without listening.

(i) A change of quality to a more lively, rhythmical motif as with a bent arm gesture, palms of hands face out away from body to meet other people—first to one side of body then the other—the body turning to contact other people in the group as the feet pick up the rhythm of the music.

(ii) The next motif involves the dancers going towards other people, using a sudden rush then stopping just away from them; turning away in order to repeat the rush to someone else.

(iii) Again 'the sound of silence' motif.

Here the group is starting to communicate but still with no real success; the first part of the whole phrase is much freer than the previous part of the dance but there is still a 'bound-flow' quality as dancers rush together then stop, turn and rush to someone else; they are holding back without actually dancing with the people they are rushing towards.

(d) Fourth verse—referring to silence growing like a cancer.

(i) The group now begins to feel a unity; all face the centre of the group gradually leaning first to one and then to the other side, slowly building up a group rhythm which culminates in everyone travelling with one side leading as the group spins on its axis.

(ii) The above phrase ends as each dancer goes into an individual spinning and everyone is spun away from the centre of the group using a high arm gesture to initiate the spin. As the group disperses the spinning slows down and ends in a sinking to the ground.

(iii) The 'sound of silence' motif follows.

The group unity has a freely-flowing quality which continues into the rest of the phrase as the group is dispersed; again it is only a brief encounter with other people.

(e) The last verse refers to worshipping the 'neon god'.

(i) Use a simple 'primitive-type' worshipping movement to build up to a frenzy: each dancer keeping on one spot, her back to the rest of the group, arms and legs jerking, head bobbing, sometimes leaping from the ground, using the rhythm of the music.

(ii) Gradually everyone is drawn together towards their 'neon god' using one point in the room as focus of attention; each dancer uses the rushing and stopping motif from earlier in the dance (getting there at different times) so that within the group some will be rushing whilst others are holding a stillness. This should be exciting and needs careful planning, leading to the climax of the dance.

(iii) The climax refers to words of prophets being written on subway walls—here the whole group move together with sudden punching arm gestures, towards the focal point again, keeping to the rhythm in the music; the punching building from low to high, stopping there, then sinking in preparation for:

(iv) The final 'sound of silence' motif.

They should be able to adapt their own 'worshipping movements' from their personal observations of primitive dancing. The climax with punching has a certain 'primitive' quality about it in contrast to the much more bound sustained finishing motif.

Composition

1 Although this can be taught as a straight study and some groups may wish to dance it as such, other groups may use the material as a basis from which to create their own group dance.

It is important that they realise how the sentiments expressed in the song have been abstracted into the medium of the dance. Point out, for example, how the 'sound of silence' motif is a movement isolating the individual from everyone else because it is very much concerned with the personal spatial sphere of the dancer. They may alter the phrases but must abstract the idea expressed in the song into dance.

2 Encourage the group to keep to the form of the composition to the extent of commencing as a solo and gradually drawing together. However, there are changes they could experiment with:

(a) All need not start at the same time or even at the same part of any given motif. Using the opening phrases of the first verse one member of a group could be dancing the small arm-circling motif—first with one side then the other side—while at the same time another member of her group is dancing with both sides together on the larger arm-circling of the 'sound of silence' motif.

(b) Rather than the haphazard way in the study, they may bring their own ideas to develop certain pathways in the second verse creating a more definite floor pattern. Again, in the third verse perhaps more than two people meeting together and then parting could develop a more definite group pattern.

(c) In verse four they may wish movement to grow differently; instead of the group travelling it could grow from low to high, or from a compact small group to a more spread-out group which will, therefore, have grown in size.

Dance subject   The sea

	Dance ideas	Analysis	Movement ideas
1	'*Moby Dick*', *by Herman Melville* one or two groups music: 'Four Sea Interludes' from 'Peter Grimes' by Benjamin Britten (background)	The power and drive of a man obsessed, to the point of madness, by the desire to overcome the whale, a symbol of the unknown. The result is a destruction of self and others. The human conflicts are set against a background of fishing activities	Main stress: quality/body. Whole body involved in pressing, wringing and slashing actions within 'hauling-in' and 'casting of nets' movements. Contrast is made with very small floating, flicking and dabbing actions in fingers and hands as nets are mended. Wringing and slashing actions may be used for situations of human conflict whilst whole group movements could use travelling, dipping and diving
2	*Storm at Sea* Group 5 music: The sea interlude 'The Storm' from 'Peter Grimes' by Benjamin Britten (close relationship)	Calm beginning increasing to rippling water being whipped up in crashing waves thrashing down on rocks. Powerful sucking and dropping back to repeat massive thrashing. Huge swell becomes overpowering	Main stress: quality/body. Whole body involved in a series of gathering and scattering movements including leaping and turning combined with slashing, wringing and pressing actions. Gradual climax is formed from a fine touch, sustained beginning. Leg gestures in leaping are stressed
3	*A Fog at Sea* Using the first stanza of the poem 'Fog' by Crosbie Garstin trio	Poetic images of a heaving, rolling mass with far-reaching tentacles which wrap around. Creeping, engulfing, clammy and cold, it slinks along like some 'foul creature'.*	Main stress: body. Whole body growing and spreading from a contracted beginning. Group also spreading and travelling to surround. Gathering movements in body and group as a preparation for gestures to flow freely outwards in different directions from the centre of the group. Group shape can swell and shrink in size as

The sea—*cont.*

it travels smoothly. Gestures of limbs curving, and group curling over and up to roll across the floor.

---

* Phrase extracted from the poem.

Development of dance idea no. 1 with teaching hints

Discussion of dance idea

The story of Moby Dick will need to be told, emphasising the obsession of one man to overcome the unknown, symbolised in the form of the whale. The 'germ idea' of the dance will be concerned with the battle between man and the unknown, man and beast, a struggle which grows into obsession in the man to the point of irrational behaviour and madness.

Reactions to the story shown by the class will be useful when working at the composition later. It may prove beneficial to ask the class to comment upon human conflicts woven into the story, and the happening of events, in an attempt to guide the children towards analysis of the novel in greater depth, and thereby arrive at possible movement ideas which encapsulate the dramatic situations in the book rather than those which act out the story line.

Work with movement ideas suggested by analysis

1 Introduce miming an action involved with fishing such as the casting or mending of nets.

Suggest repetition of action a few times to clarify the rhythm of the action, its preparation into the action and recovery with an accent placed on the action.

2 Whilst the children are repeating the action, draw their attention to body shape created during the action and the relationship between one body part and the next, for example, the use of hands in the action, or of movement and positioning of feet.

These movement ideas are relevant for future dance motifs which, at present, are in 'mime' form.

3 Encourage enlargement of the action so that the whole body becomes involved in the movement and moves in a greater area of space.

> This is one further step towards developing a dance motif from a miming action.

4 Encourage any body activities, such as jumping, turning, travelling, etc which could develop from the directions indicated in the mimed action. For example, a rising gesture of the knees could develop into a jumping motif, or a gesture sideways of elbows could develop into an opening or closing turn of the whole body.

> This again is a way of developing the dance motif from the mimed action.

5 The rhythmic content of the action, emphasised earlier through repetition, will now have been clarified and developed further by enlarging the size of the movement and developing the body actions inherent in the action. The accent in the movement needs emphasising clearly, so that the phrase which could result from repeating the preparation and leading into the accented action followed by the recovery is also clearly formed.

> One of the accents could be more strongly placed than the others, thereby giving a climax to the phrase.

6 Clarity of rhythmic content also involves clarity in effort actions, and the transitions from one to another within an action.

> The shape inherent in each effort action should also be clear as the pupils should be capable of achieving this without much prompting. For example, a slashing turn into a thrusting retreating movement should be accompanied by a twisted shape in the body followed by a linear shape.

7 Use of the body could be experimented with. The parts of the body emphasised in the action could be replaced by others, for example, hands grasping may be replaced by feet grasping. Or if the whole body is used in the mimetic action, the movement, as a dance motif, could be performed by one small part of the body; a throwing action in the whole body may be performed by the lower leg only taking on the throwing action, and using similar qualities and rhythmic content.

> These suggestions are, in fact, variations of the original actions being explored using the body in a way which is unusual to real and practical situations, and which tends to

be more exciting, imaginative and original, with a feeling of illusion about it.

8 Each fishing action suggested by the class and teacher can be treated in a similar manner which transforms the occupation action into a dance motif.

Encourage the use of the trunk and centre of the body in whole body movements, so that the dance motif is danced with full expression.

Play the music as the children work so that the rhythms are enhanced and phrasing and qualities of movements are further clarified.

9 Having acquired as rich a movement vocabulary as possible, centred on the dance idea chosen for the composition, the children could work on improvisations concerned with group shapes and group formations stimulated by the idea of chase and the battle ensuing.

The music could accompany the improvisations, enhancing the qualities and moods of the dance movements.

Suggestions for group formations from the class could be encouraged, such as leaders and pursuers against the pursued, if two groups are being used. Pursuers could be individuals forming one group shape which may change and travel, surface and submerge.

Interactions between the two groups can come from the pupils being stimulated by the dramatic situations arising from the human conflicts between men and between the man and the whale.

There is a danger for the children to mime rather than dance, copy rather than abstract and transform. It is therefore necessary for the teacher to encourage involvement of the whole body, particularly the body centre, in the movements, enlarging them, rhythmising and phrasing them.

Composition

The aim of the group dance is not to narrate, step by step the story of Moby Dick, but rather to abstract the essence of the story, that is, the analysis of the dance idea, and transform it into a dance form by using the imagination to create movement ideas which embody and express the dance idea.

1 Organise the groups in whatever way the dancers have de-

cided to work. Suggest that initially they all begin using fishing motifs either in unison or in canon, or question and answer form if they are divided into two groups.

These motifs will have been selected from the previous improvisations.

2   The fishing motifs need to be repeated to allow variations to occur.

It may be best to concentrate on repeating, clarifying and varying motifs, and to organise the material into dance phrases before introducing any new material through development.

3   Suggest that the fishing motif could vary and develop into one which creates conflict and unrest between the leader and the group, or between two groups.

The music can accompany whenever and wherever the teacher feels it will be of most value in sweeping the children along in their dance.

Work on the composition will involve ideas such as the power of one man driving a group onwards, a leader becoming obsessed with the notion of conquering the unknown—the whale (the pursued group).

4   Motifs need to be developed, from the previous ones in the composition, to incorporate new material embodying the ideas of chasing to destroy, a driving power urging an individual onwards to the point of self-destruction and destruction of others. Attack and counterattack, or defence could develop between the hunters and the whale. The whale group could dance maintaining contact throughout, thereby achieving a high degree of group sensitivity as the group 'whale-shape' alters in response to the attackers and moves, dipping, diving, rising up and plunging down, over, under, towards and away from the attackers.

The above suggestions are only a few of the possible situations the group could create and develop.

The teacher needs to encourage selection of movement situations within and between the groups, which the groups consider to be workable and appropriate to the analysis of the dance idea.

5   After creating the illusion of the conflict, the groups need to resolve the situation. Ask for suggestions from the class for ways of resolving the tensions built up, and ways of developing

and completing the aesthetic form of the dance, to avoid stringing a series of events depicted in the story line.

The composition should evolve along lines determined by a particular kind of 'inner logic' inherent in the dance symbol, the work of art. Variations and developments of motifs and their organisation and manipulation need to be such that 'rightness and necessity' are created by their presence at a particular place and time in the composition. The same thing goes for the group formations used and the various relationships that are created throughout the composition. The children should be made very aware of this sensitivity towards 'rightness and necessity' in the composing of the dance.

6 Finally give opportunity for the dance compositions to be performed a few times by the groups, so that the children may experience and master the techniques involved in their dance, and to allow for full appreciation and criticism of the dance form they have created as a work of art.

Dance subject   Clothes

	Dance ideas	Analysis	Movement ideas
1	*Variety of hats, eg bowler, sunhat, top-hat etc* solo	(a) Shape and design of hat, eg oval, squat, rounded, pointed. (b) Texture and colour, eg vivid, gay, dull, severe, woolly, knobbly, smooth, hard etc. (c) Association of characters who wear the hats, eg businessman in his bowler moving briskly, or leisurely sunhat, motor cyclists helmet	Main stress: spatial/quality. An example. Sunhat— curved shapes in step pattern and in body shape and gestures. Qualities of free flow, sustainment and fine touch. Movements extending away from centre of body and returning to centre combined with rotations of trunk of body
2	*Effects of skirts or cloaks on movement of the body* group: 5	Short tight skirts with mincing walks, knees held close together, contrasted with long skirts flowing and being shaped by leg move-	Main stress: quality/body. Sudden, bound-flow, fine-touch qualities in stepping with variations in direction. Attention on legs and feet, large leg gestures

Clothes—*cont.*

		ments in stepping. Elegant and swirling. Flowing circles could be transferred to shoulder levels to include unfolding and wrapping round, swirling and swishing of a cloak enveloping the body	imitating scattering movements into turning, followed by gathering movements interplay with contrasting firm, freely flowing strides. Arm gestures echo the scattering and gathering whilst the body turns, sinks and rises. Pauses held when body gathered in, suddenly to be released in slashing turns and free flow travelling
3	*Shoes—different types eg wellington boots, ballet and tap shoes, fashion shoes, clogs* solo	Heavy boots drag the legs down. Large clumsy and strong movements. Ballet shoes lead to delicate, vital, precise and rhythmic movements. Fashion shoes are dignified, careful movements	Main stress: quality/body. Large leg gestures with firm quality. Uses of feet stressed. Sustained deliberate stepping, contrasted with dab-like steps mainly on toes, and body held upright. Rhythmic heel and toe movements of tap shoes using a sudden quality. Floor patterns emphasised

Development of dance idea no. 1 with teaching hints

Discussion of dance idea

Encourage the class to bring hats of their own choice which will appeal to each individual and which will help gain their interest and involvement. The hat will be worn initially.

Focus their attention upon the 'character' of the hat and the reason for their choice. Ask them to write or verbally describe to a partner their hat, its characteristic properties, shape, texture and associations of ideas, such as round, large, brimmed, frilly, solid. Begin by considering some of the descriptive 'shape' words as stimuli for improvisations on shapes in movement, such as body shapes, shapes in air and floor patterns.

Work with movement ideas suggested by analysis

1   From the shape of the hat being worn, encourage the children to experiment with that shape in floor patterns and in body shape.

For example, a sunhat with a large brim could stimulate improvisations on circular pathways traced on the floor in stepping, or the body could take on a spreading into a curve shaped movement which involves gestures of arms and legs. Encourage rapid experimentation on varied ideas rather than focusing on one idea.

This is so that a richer fund of movements is available for selection during composition.

2 Still retaining the clear pathways in travelling, introduce clear air patterns in which gestures trace out relevant shapes to the hat ideas discussed earlier. The type of hat will determine the shapes and designs the body creates in space; a sunhat could result in gathering and scattering movements of the whole body and rotations in the body with arms held spread.

One needs to be wary of mimetic movement continuing for too long, and one must therefore encourage larger trunk movements to accompany any gestures of limbs.

Improvisations could be accompanied by music if it is being used as background to the dance.

3 Draw the class's attention to the textures of the hat and any decoration or pattern on it.

The textures of the hat can stimulate a combination of qualities and shapes in the movements of the body.

Some hats easily suggest shapes in movement, others textures, for example, knobbly-textured hats could involve joints and bony parts of the body gesturing in tight, twisting movements. Fists could play a prominent part. The qualities of the movements could be flexibility with interplays of suddenness and sustainment.

4 If there is a pattern in the fabric of the hat, the shape-design aspects of the pattern could be utilised in stimulating movements of the body which involve similar shapes. By using repetition movement patterns could evolve, sparked off by the hat patterns. Variations could be incorporated in the repeated movements such as shaping the motif in the hands, then echoing the shape in stepping patterns of the feet or gestures of other parts of the body.

The establishing of a pattern involves the use of repetition, and in movement this can be achieved by repeating the same shapes in the body with different parts of the body, repeating the air patterns, floor patterns or rhythmic patterns.

5   There may spring to mind an association of ideas related to
the particular type of hat, for example a bowler hat is connected
with the image of a businessman with his upright carriage and
efficient, brisk quality of movement. This could lead to a phrase of
movement incorporating small, sudden steps which change direction sharply or gestures of the upper part of the body which trace
angular air patterns through the space around the body. Similar
shapes can be created with the whole body by emphasising the
joints of the body to make angular movements.

Hats may or may not be worn at this stage. Wearing a
particular hat does influence the movements of the body,
but can also limit the extent of the movements.

It is advisable to use only the association of ideas which
have action possibilities conducive to movement ideas.

6   Some types of hats can, through association of ideas, create
specific atmospheres, for example, a sunhat tends to suggest
leisurely easygoing movements. Ask the children to describe the
mood which could be stimulated using 'quality' words. Adjectives
can more easily find their counterpart in movement; the sunhat
could create a sultry, languid, lazy mood in which movements
would probably involve very sustained floating and gliding
actions. Curved shapes in the body and in air and floor patterns,
uninterrupted, lend themselves to an effect of smoothness and
peacefulness.

Composition

1   In the section above, improvisations have been suggested
based on (a), (b), (c) aspects of the dance idea as seen in the
analysis. Suggest to the class that either aspect (a), (b) or (c) forms
the basis of their compositions. Aspect (c) need not enter into the
composition at all, or it may be the main idea of the dance.

2   Suggest that the children study their own hats again in the
light of their improvisations, and depending on the emphasis
they have decided to lay on aspect (a), (b) or (c) in their dance,
encourage them to recall, work on, and develop, repeat and
clarify their ideas, stimulated by either the shape and dseign of
the hat, or the texture, colour, patterns or an association with a
character who wears the hat.

This is where the child will select from the fund of movements improvised upon earlier and referred to in the teach-

ing points under paragraph *1* of *work with movement ideas.*

3 Help the children to create dance motifs appropriate for their hat dance, selected from the earlier improvisations, by manipulating their material using any part or all the body, moving on the floor and away from it, discarding movements or changing parts of movements so that shapes, designs, textures, quality and rhythmic content of the motifs begin to emerge and are seen to encapsulate their dance ideas. Repetition to consolidate and clarify motifs is then necessary.

> Motifs should form the 'seed' from which the dance composition grows. It is therefore vital that the teacher encourages richness in movement ideas from the children's improvisations earlier on. It is always tempting to accept the first movements which spring to mind and body without pursuing one's thoughts further and working one's imagination and body to their limits. This is a stage also when 'corny' movements slip in which may be relevant, but which merely 'pad' out the dance rather than enrich it and further its development.

4 Suggest that each child selects two contrasting motifs A and B, for example, one may be concerned with the shape and design of the hat, the other with the type of person who could wear it. Interesting relationships between hat and dancer could arise and perhaps lead to a comic dance. The hat need not be worn in the final composition. It could be discarded once the selection of motifs has occurred.

> It facilitates the process of composition if the children work with strongly contrasting motifs, for they seem to be able to create and experience kinaesthetically the relationships between the two motifs, and they are more easily able to develop their material.

5 Through repetition, encourage variations of motif A, gradually building the motif and variations into dance phrases. Suggest that a climax is made within the phrases to shape them. One or more phrases can be composed.

> Repetition of a motif too many times without any variation becomes monotonous and 'dead'.

6 Perform the original motif A followed by the contrasting

motif B, and repeat these two motifs together several times so that the contrasts between them are clarified. Then return to motif A and its variation(s) phrase. The whole section is therefore as follows:

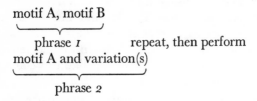

motif A, motif B

phrase *1*   repeat, then perform
motif A and variation(s)

phrase *2*

   At least two phrases should have been performed.

7   Suggest that any part of the section just performed is selected for the beginnings of a development phrase *3*. The selected part could be as small as a slight turn of the head or a shuffle in the feet or a tilt of the trunk of the body. Repeat the movement(s) a few times, gradually varying the movements. Then suggest that a new movement is introduced which has not been seen before in the composition but which has some relationship with the movement selected from the previous section. For example, a shuffle in the feet could increase in speed (variation) gradually involving the whole body in a vibratory movement, which the arms and fists take over and decelerate with a shunting movement. This movement develops, finally, into a sustained, firm pulling-away from each other, and coming together in an interlocking of fists phrase perhaps—a very different flavour from the shuffling feet, and yet developed from it.

8   Now motif B could be varied in a similar way to motif A, and built into a phrase shaped by climax(es).

   Each child should now have composed a phrase, incorporating motif A and motif B, phrase *2* incorporating motif A and its variation(s), phrase *3* as the development phrase and phrase *4* with motif B and variation(s).

9   With this material, encourage each pupil to organise the phrases into a structured whole, a form in which one phrase flows on to the next with some feeling for movement continuity and inherent logic.

   Not all the material need be used. Parts of phrases may be selected and other parts rejected if it results in a more aesthetically satisfying product. The judge of that is ultimately the teacher, who must try to develop an awareness of what is aesthetically satisfying and complete in form.

10   Once the compositions are complete, the teacher needs to give opportunity for each child to dance her composition and for the other children to observe the finished composition and critically appraise it with help from the teacher. Discussion following can be most fruitful if it is guided towards observations of the aesthetic form of the composition. For example, some pupils watching may feel that the dance they have been observing has not reached its logical conclusion and its form is incomplete, others may be more concerned with particular motifs and the originality of these.

Particular questions asked by the teacher can be such that the children need to draw on their powers of observation to answer them, in such a way as to result in each pupil developing an aesthetic appreciation of her own and other pupils' work.

Dance subject   Growth

	Dance ideas	Analysis	Movement ideas
1	'*Mushrooms*' *A poem by Sylvia Plath* Can be read aloud during the dance group	From a small beginning a growing and expanding of each person and group causing a crowding and eventual expansion until the group shape is spread to its extremities	Main stress: relationship/body. A tiny movement initiates a gradual spreading, a 'nudging' and 'shoving' with rhythmical elbows shoulders, etc. Passing other people then spreading with others, increasing size and moving more freely in space to spread the group as far as possible
2	'*Circle Game*' *by Joni Mitchell* (a folk song from her album 'The Ladies of the Canyon') group	Simple expression of the words of the song, almost mime, beginning alone then group in unison for chorus; as child grows older more complicated relationships an inevitability of circles going round	Main stress: relationships. Circular group formations in which body flow is most important, leaning to one side then the other, travelling around and up and down 'captured on a carousel of time'. Starts as a solo, then pairs, into

Growth—*cont.*

3 *A Study from a Small Beginning*

group

music: 'Bolero' by Ravel

(close relationship)

(close relationship)

increasing in size as chorus is repeated

A small beginning by one person which is an indication of the study. As the music is repeated so the movement grows and eventually the phrase is complete and can be repeated in full. Meanwhile other groups have begun, at different times, only when last person has reached the full phrase can the dance be completed

fours, into eights then larger group
Main stress: body. Standing upright one shoulder indicates the forward diagonal closed low direction; then other shoulder. From these two directions a study can be built using a stepping pattern to the clear rhythm of the Bolero, eg right foot steps forward across body. *1* left foot steps back, *2* right foot back and to the side, *3* repeat on the other diagonal. Arms indicate diagonals and can gesture forward low and then backwards high over head. Once the phrase has been mastered the simple growth in the relationship can be experimented with ie each person in the group starts the study at a different time and there is a gradual growth into a full study

Development of dance idea no. 1 with teaching hints

Discussion of dance idea

Read the poem to the class then start discussion by reference to the dance subject 'Growth' and in what way this is indicated in the poem. The growth is slow, small but insistent and by the end of the poem it is suggested they shall 'inherit the earth'. Certain images in the poem might stimulate movement, for example, 'our toes or our noses take hold on the loam, acquire the air' and 'soft fists insist on heaving the needles'. Movement possibilities can arise from the words describing mushrooms as 'shelves' and 'tables'. Discuss how these shapes can lead into movement, for example, spreading turning in the shape of a table, and a rising upwards then a curving over like a shelf. 'Nudgers and shovers' gives plenty of opportunity for movement.

Work with movement ideas suggested by analysis

1 Start working as a solo improvising on verses 1 and 2.

(a) Suggest they vary parts of the body close to the ground and the body gradually expands growing away from the ground.

(b) They could take a 'mushroom' shape close to the ground with back bent and expand from there, the whole body lifting perhaps with a rising, sinking, rising. Or from the mushroom, different body parts 'acquire the air' gradually spreading.

> Help the gradual expansion by starting small and feeling which part of their anatomy must move first in order to commence their movement; it may be necessary for the shoulders to have the initiative in the rising, sinking phrase or the hips may initiate the movement, adjusting the balance of the body as it gradually expands away from the ground. Background music could be very useful here, for example, 'Breathe' from 'Dark Side of the Moon' by Pink Floyd, it might also help if the poem is read to the class as they dance, encouraging them to start slowly.

2 Verses 4, 5 and 6 express a stronger quality. Request class to gradually increase the strength of their original 'growing' motifs at the same time drawing together in twos or threes ending this phrase in a unison movement.

> There will be an increase of tension in the body—perhaps an increase in size of movement—as they travel towards each other and the unison movement, improvised at first, is a more powerful statement than a solo movement.

3 Verses 7 and 8—each group should work on a unison motif which may develop from their first unison movement but should contain a rising and spreading and be more freely flowing although not too complicated since by the end of verse 8—'so many of us!'—they should vary their motif to meet other groups.

> It might help to limit this motif to one body part, such as shoulders, which could lift the body and then initiate a turning to spread the group. It should not be necessary for

any group to travel far to meet other groups—the common task of rising and spreading should bring them together if they are aware of what is happening to other groups.

4   Verse 9—once the larger groups have been established, ask whether they wish to take either 'shelves', 'tables' or 'meek'. Discuss movement possibilities within these three words.

(a) Shelves—a narrow rising with protruding angles, perhaps the group on different levels and facing in different directions.

(b) Tables—a flat spreading, smoothing at waist level which can go into turning (either individually or the group as a whole) and could encircle one large 'table' showing the shape of a mushroom.

(c) Meek—a bowing over, cowering movement has for centuries been an expression of meekness—their phrase must end in stillness.

They may wish to try out all three ideas before choosing. This part of the dance could take up the larger part of a lesson and be much more freely flowing than the previous part. Encourage retention of something of their original motifs to help keep the composition harmonious.

5   Verse 10—'Nudgers and Shovers'. Starting from stillness, one person in the room begins to 'nudge and shove' people close to her infecting the rest of the class which is gradually drawn into one tight group with shoulders touching—shoulders should be stressed in the 'nudging'.

This movement will have grown through the entire group stressing the phrase 'our kind multiplies'.

6   From this climax there should be a menacing note introduced; perhaps a slow advancing of the whole group. Or still keeping contact, but with fingers rather than shoulders, the group gradually spread to 'inherit the earth'.

The end should have a sombre quality which may be effected by moving slowly and deliberately, perhaps increasing in strength to give a feeling of power.

Composition

1   The overall form of the dance has already been sketched in by the teacher using the poem as a stimulus for the group formations and relationships. The class develop their own motifs within the framework and should be able to repeat and vary them within the

given relationships in order that one part of the composition grows naturally into the next part.

2 Once the dance has been completed ask for suggestions of other endings suitable—referring back to the last verse of the poem:

> 'We shall by morning
> Inherit the earth,
> One foot's in the door.'

Discussion could arise as to the poet's intention. Why so menacing at the end? Is it only mushrooms she is talking about? From these discussions the class could be encouraged to add their own ideas to the composition.

3 The class could decide whether it is necessary for the poem to be spoken as it is danced and whether they would prefer music in the background to complement the poem.

Chapter 6

Dance Ideas for 15-16 year Age Group

In the fifth year, dance does not always appear as a subject in the school curriculum or on the school timetable, and often has to continue in the form of a physical education option or a club.

If dance is not taught continuously throughout the school, many of the pupils who opt for it in the fifth year may not have danced for some time, if at all. A separate section, in this chapter, has been included to deal with the problems of introducing dance to senior girls for the first time.

However, dance ideas do need to be varied in content to cater for those children who have pursued dance throughout the school. Fifth-year pupils enjoy involving themselves in very varied dance moods resulting from contrasting dance ideas but not involving great depths of research. For example, dance ideas such as the 'characterisation of Madame Défarge', '*Ennui*, a painting by Sickert', or the myth 'Orpheus in the Underworld', all of which call for changes of mood to be experienced by the children.

There also needs to be a variety of methods of presentation in the teaching, the methods being closely linked with a strong need for balance between creative and interpretive work. Both demand involvement and concentration of different kinds, the latter requiring acute powers of observation in reproducing a study or choreographed dance, and in giving one's own interpretation of the set movements. Dance ideas should call upon methods of presentation ranging from the teacher composing most of a dance and leaving a section for the pupils to complete using their own resources and imaginations (see, for example, dance idea 'Dancing Clown') to dance ideas being presented as stimuli for improvisations and further creative work. In the latter case the teacher will need to guide the children towards their own style of artistic expression rather than give her own suggestions. The directed dance study and the choreographed dance, completed by the teacher, are ways of presenting to the children learning situations which are a contrast to situations demanding purely creative work, and which demand mastery and reproduction of specific movements.

Fifth-form pupils are becoming more aware of themselves in varied roles. They seem to be experiencing their own adolescent struggles and problems. They begin to see world problems as real fragments of life which can impinge upon those who are sensitive to them. This seems to be the age of sensitivity. The pupils often find stimulating material for dance ideas in human conflicts and problems common to most communities such as fights for independence and freedom. Dance ideas need to concern themselves with such concepts as man's efforts to break the bonds of his human limitations, to perform the humanly impossible and to seek explanations for things which defy reason. This is very closely related to the sentiments of mythology, where man creates myth in order to explain the unexplained areas of his life, which also presents a rich source of material for dance ideas.

Fifth-year pupils can become very involved with phenomena in the world. They enjoy discussing stories in newspapers which involve unexplainable events. The object of mythology is to explain the phenomena in the world. It has always been material for poets and philosophers, from ancient man to modern times, from every civilisation. The presentation of the legends and fables often appeals to and stimulates a group of this age which is capable of involving itself with the kind of concepts expressed in legends and fables. The examples of dance ideas given under the dance subject 'Greek Mythology' have been selected for their most apparent links with certain aspects of movement. For example, 'Icarus and Daedalus' can utilise tipping and tilting of the body, flying and jumping movements, not to mention the changes of mood and underlying moral which the myth expresses.

At fifth-year level pupils seem to enjoy suggesting and working on their own dance ideas, solving the choreographic problems which arise. This way of working should be encouraged by the teacher as it is the very attitude she should be trying to develop.

The pupils of this age often express a desire to complete and polish dances which they themselves have composed, and which

they then enjoy dancing through a number of times. Dance ideas
such as 'Lazy' offer these opportunities. Dance ideas, concerned
with directed dance studies, should have clear aesthetic form and
expression as both these aspects are greatly appreciated by this
age group.

Overall there is a rejuvenation of spontaneity in the children's
responses to dance ideas, and in their energies to carry them
through for dance compositions. Although mastering of skill and
technique is enjoyed, the pupils also enjoy experiencing the sensation of action, and the relationship between the two.

By the fifth year the inhibitions of the previous two years
should have been replaced by a desire to 'have a go'. Dance ideas
involving the sensations of flying and falling movements, of being
off-balance, tipping and tilting, can be fully explored. Such ideas
as 'Icarus and Daedalus' under dance subject 'Greek Mythology' incorporate movement sensations with the possible movement ideas gathered from the analysis of the dance idea. The
dance idea also presents the movement material in a form palat-
able to the fifth-year pupil. It not only involves the actions of
jumping, turning and gesturing, but also the sensations of elevation, flying and falling, and the challenge to break the bonds of
gravity and conquer the human limitations by flying.

There also exists, within this dance idea, the love between
father and son, the guidance of one and the learning of the other
with the disobedience of the impetuous youth. The myth involves
strong changes of mood from exhilarating triumph to deepest
grief. This dance idea represents only a small part of the world of
mythology, and it is only used here to show how vital it is for the
dance ideas, for any age group, to satisfy more than the need to
experience a wide movement vocabulary.

In both their creative and study work the pupils should show
a further increase in the clarity of orientating their movements in
space. Dance subjects and related dance ideas, such as 'clowns',
attempt to utilise this skill, and many other dance ideas could be
introduced to achieve similar learning situations.

The pupils are also capable of further abstractions using spatially stressed dance ideas. They are beginning to understand
something of the interplays between one shape and the next, such
as curve to curve, line crossing line. Spatial designs are also beginning to appeal as possible stimuli for dance compositions, for

example, dance idea 'Madame Défarge' under dance subject 'Characterisation'.

The fifth year is also the age when a sensitivity between members of a group is achieved. Group dances of any number where social adaptations are emphasised can be worked upon. Dance ideas should cater for these needs by offering learning situations in which group relationships change within the dance, see, for example, dance ideas under dance subject 'Moods'.

Dance ideas can utilise group formations such as linear forms in which lines can cross, separate, form barriers, weave, encircle and spiral, yet maintain group relationships within the formation. The concept of the circle is also grasped. The circle shape can not only contract, extend and surround, but it is a unit in which all its members have an equal part to play. There is no leader. There is also the ritual significance of the circle which can be used in compositions by the pupils, working on their own.

The fifth-year classes seem to welcome the opportunity to discuss the content of dance ideas, and the significance of the particular group formation which may have arisen in their compositions. Now, one can expect much more conceptualisation in the development of dances, and one can introduce dances with a 'meaning' as pupils grasp the idea that an artist often wants to 'say' something through his creation.

The significance of block group formations is another area for exploration. For example, if the block advances, the dancers moving in unison, it becomes a confrontation, almost threatening in its solidarity as mass response in unison gives the formation power. As soon as the block narrows at one side to form a wedge shape or spearhead, there is assumed a penetrating, attacking mood. Such group formation work is most useful in dance dramas where more than dancing through a story should occur. A comment on the dramatic situation should be made by the group. This is referred to in the composition section.

Fifth-form pupils can also create irregular group formations in their compositions which should relate to and enhance the initial dance idea.

Composition

Fifth-form pupils need an explanation of what lies behind a specific dance idea in greater depth than previous years have needed. They seem to have much to offer, in discussion, which could be used in their compositions later. Discussions within the dance lessons can be seen to satisfy this need and, if the teacher can stimulate interest and motivate the group, dance compositions should appear with inspiration and life.

The pupils at this stage do enjoy experiencing a harmony within the movements of their dances, whether the dances are choreographed by the teacher or composed by themselves. They also appreciate a clear form in the composition and clear artistic expression. However, in their own group-work most of them are unable to produce such clarity of aesthetic form, even though the feeling for 'rightness' and necessity of motifs within phrases being played off one against the other is beginning to develop. Their dances may appear formless, even though the pupils will often be able to comment upon spatial patterns they see emerging within their own group dances.

Their dances, however, are lengthening as material is being developed and extended. The pupils are beginning to show an ability to manipulate dance material using repetition, variations and development to produce a satisfying dance composition.

It is important that the teacher brings to the understanding of the pupils involved in dance composition at this stage the importance of seeking and creating a 'germ-cell'—from which all else grows and which has been stimulated by the chosen dance idea. The process of dance composition does not involve narrating nor copying, in movement terms, what is stated in other art forms; rather it involves the creating of illusions and impressions which are embodied in the dance form and which give the dance its import.

After initial stimulation from the dance idea resulting in improvisation, motivation in the pupils often dwindles, and the desire to continue the 'nitty-gritty' of composition is dampened. It is at this moment in the children's learning that the teacher must play her greatest and most difficult part in encouraging and guiding the pupils through their work to achieve fruition without overdominance and indoctrination of her own idea.

Music

As varied a selection of music as possible is necessary so that the pupils' knowledge of using music with dance is broadened, deepened and enriched all round. Further detail is given in chapter 8 on music for dance, where special reference is made to the fifth year.

Introducing dance as a new subject to seniors

There are many reasons why teachers find themselves introducing dance as a new subject to senior classes. It may be offered as an option within the PE syllabus or as a subject for the Certificate of Secondary Education. Over the last few years there has been an increase in enthusiasm for dance and many senior girls are genuinely interested but have not had previous dance lessons. Their knowledge of dance is often limited to what they have seen on television, but teachers will find it both stimulating and challenging to teach these classes. From our experience we have found girls eager to learn and to share in our own enthusiasm for dance and, by using appropriate dance subjects, they have quickly become involved in creating their own dances.

Dance subjects chosen for this specific purpose will introduce creative work gradually; the chief function will be to get the class moving in what they can recognise as a dance form. They are aware of dance as a conventional way of moving in a certain situation, such as ballroom dancing and, at the other end of the scale, primitive dance. Dance subjects utilising these conventions help them to feel secure. The material must be simple enough bodily to give them confidence in their own performance; only when some technique has been developed will they be able to reveal themselves in a creative way.

The simplest way to teach technique or body actions to this age group is by the 'observe and do' method. Set study/steps will help reduce any embarrassment besides helping to develop technique. Motifs need to be clear within a conventional formation but, right from the beginning, some part of the dance must be left for them to develop, such as completing a given phrase or motif, or organising the given motifs together. We feel there is very little artistic experience for beginners if they are pushed through complete pre-choreographed dances. Therefore, in all the dance subjects suggested as suitable introduction dances to seniors there is an element of set study/steps to help technique and to give the class something concrete from which to work, but added to this there should be an opportunity to contribute something of themselves.

The age of the pupils must be taken into consideration when introducing them to dance. These older girls want more sophisticated dance subjects but need very specific help with movement ideas and choreography. The teacher should use the correct terms for work they are doing giving the impression they are learning a new subject and are enabled to join in discussion right from the start. By the end of the first few lessons they should be able to make harmonious and controlled movements, which flow from the trunk of the body outwards to the limbs. The basic vocabulary helps to increase their self-confidence as their knowledge increases.

Some sort of accompaniment is needed as they are used to dancing to music and, on the whole, like to stick to conventions. Music helps them shape and phrase their movements. We found rhythmical drumming (taped) successful as the rhythm swept the girls along much the same way as it would dancers of a primitive tribe (see dance subject 'Characteristics of Primitive Dancing'). As experience grows necessity for musical accompaniment decreases; indeed they should not become dependent upon music for rhythm alone. Some modern popular groups, such as 'Pink Floyd', are producing music with a great variety of sound and rhythm, very suitable for dance and, of course, popular with the older pupils.

It is very important for the teacher to be part of the group when introducing dance at this level, building up the confidence of the group around her enthusiasm. It will be necessary for her to dance with the group for at least part of the time—particularly at the beginning of the lesson—having everyone dancing at the same time and no one feeling conspicuous. A circle formation (led by the teacher) often helps build up a group relationship as the girls will be aware of each other as equals working together and overcoming any embarrassment together. We offered dance to seniors as an option within the PE curriculum and found that girls who had contributed little to other branches of PE were very happy to dance once confidence and a certain degree of understanding of what they were expected to do were gained.

Dance subject   Clowns
(Suitable for beginners)

	Dance ideas	Analysis	Movement ideas
1	*Dancing clown**

duo

music: 'The Entertainer' by Scott Joplin

(background) | Lively, amusing using the antics of a clown as a basis for dance motifs. Relationships include chasing, some slapstick | Main stress: body. Funny walks, arresting movement, exaggerated gestures increase and decrease in size of movement. Quality of surprise —sudden stops and changes |
| 2 | *Romanticised clown*

solo

music: 'Pierrot' from *Carnaval* by Schumann

(background) | Sad, foolish man with awkward movements trips over own feet, etc. seeking the unattainable | Main stress: quality. Slow clumsy movements into sudden picking up of feet to recover— reaching out into space and then crumpling up. Attempting more complicated steps |
| 3 | *Slapstick*

group: with props

music: loud brass band

(background) | Group chasing, stopping falling over. A chain routine passed around the group— falling off, etc. Exaggerated fighting, dodging and recovering | Main stress: body/relationships. Using the clown-like dance motifs within a group. Contrasting characters using natural relationships, eg slow lumbering 'clown' following a lively energetic 'clown' |

* Suitable as an introductory lesson for older girls

Development of dance idea no. 1 with teaching hints

Discussion of dance idea

Discuss what makes a movement clown-like. One main factor is exaggeration, as in the enormous strides clowns take when chasing each other. Also some actions are exaggerated by the length of time taken—the slowing down of a throwing action as in a 'custard-pie' scene, or the speeding up of recovery in a fall. For some reason these exaggerations are amusing to watch. Unexpected happenings also cause hilarity. A sudden fall, a chair collapsing under a clown, or a bucket of 'water', which when thrown at the audience is full of bits of paper. All these unexpected things shock the audience into laughter. Clowns also use repetition to stress peculiarities—the jerk of a knee in an otherwise normal walk becomes amusing when repeated, also it is often very rhythmical, as in, for example, the distinctive 'funny-walks' used by Charlie Chaplin and Max Wall.

Work on movement ideas suggested by analysis

1   Funny walks.

(a) Start the class walking around the room in an ordinary way then ask them to make up their own 'funny walks' using any of the methods previously discussed.

(b) Play music quietly in the background which may help anyone inhibited.

(c) If some are without ideas suggest they develop a 'Charlie Chaplin' walk, ie heels turned in and arms swinging a stick.

(d) They should be able to repeat their walk, know the direction they take and have clear gestures in their body, for example, elbows bent in an exaggerated running action.

> It may be necessary to stipulate one particular stress, either body or quality, in order to help them clarify their 'walk'. Their walk may be interrupted by a slow-motion 'trip-up' followed by a fall ending in a sudden recovery back to standing—in this case the time quality is more important than which part of the body first lands on the floor. In another phrase the gestures of knees and elbows may be the most important aspect. Experienced classes would be able to clarify body and quality.

2   With a partner they could observe each other's 'walk' then copy one another, dancing together. Add one walk to the other and choose their relationships, for example, face each other and dance towards each other—back to back to each other—one behind the other.

> By now their 'walk' should be a clear stepping pattern. By observation they can gain extra ideas from one another and become aware of how they have developed their 'walk'.

3   A short study—using the polka-type step favoured by many clowns and comedians as part of their acts.

(a) Facing front, right leg takes a large gesture before stepping to the side (one); left foot joins right foot (two); and there is another shorter step to the right side (three), ie a polka step to the side with the first leg gesture emphasised.

(b) Repeat to the other side (left leg having the exaggerated gesture).

(c) Stress the very lively and energetic quality clowns put into this step, feet turned up, knees turned out and head jutting forward—Max Wall has an undulation in the trunk of his body as he dances this step.

(d) A variation of the above step—which would be possible with some classes—has a heel kicking up behind after the large gesture to the side, that is right leg gesture and step, left heel kick up behind before stepping to join right foot.

This is only one example of a study which could be used. Other steps the teacher has devised for herself could be used in this part of the lesson; or use a step invented by one of the class at the beginning of the lesson.

4 Add the study (3 above) to the previous partner work (2 above) making three clear motifs.

(a) Each person's own motif (A and B).

(b) The study (C).

Leave class to improvise with A, B and C.

This could be the basis of a simple composition, trying to keep them aware of relationships, for example, does one follow the other or are they dancing towards each other?

5 Slapstick.

(a) Work on an action involving a large, sweeping arm gesture which spins the body around, perhaps finishing suddenly or perhaps slowing down. The spin could end with the body close to the floor or high away from the floor; slow motion might exaggerate the action.

(b) A kicking leg gesture carrying the body forwards and ending in a hopping around is another possible way of developing a clown-action into something more dance-like.

(c) Exaggerated 'trip-up and fall-down' occurring in many clown acts could be analysed and a suitable dance phrase developed. The rhythm of the stepping and the gestures in the tripping will be important. Falling down could be a sudden or a gradual process; the surprise element of the fall will be very important and parts of the phrase could be repeated to add a more dance-like element.

(d) Clutching buttocks to denote a kick from a partner—one hand takes a sweeping gesture to the buttock, the other hand has a similar gesture repeating the same rhythm, followed by a succession of steps with hands on buttocks as hips sway from side to side; the whole phrase can be repeated.

It is most important the class realise they are abstracting ideas from clown movements to develop into a dance and that they are not acting-out clowns; they need to add other elements such as rhythm and quality. It should be noted that some of the best clown performers (Charlie Chaplin, Jacques Tati) have a dance element in their actions.

Composition

1   It is necessary to discuss with the partner the ideas they are going to select for their composition. During discussion point out to the class the possibilities to which this dance idea may lend itself.

(a) The dramatic approach, that is, a clown act with tricks, chasing, slapstick and so on.

(b) A more lyrical approach using previous phrases, linking them together and forming a composition which will include amusing movements—the essence of clowning rather than the tricks.

2   Each dancer could work on her own separate motifs, thus developing two different characters; or the couple may choose to dance the same motifs, not necessarily dancing in unison nor perhaps starting at the same point of the phrase each time.

3   The relationship should be kept simple to be in character with the dance idea—a clown's act is not usually sophisticated;

(a) they may dance—
    (i) side by side.
    (ii) one behind the other.
    (iii) facing each other.

(b) The 'question and answer' simple choreographic idea would suit this dance, as one dances her phrase and finishes (question) the other replies with her phrase (answer). Action/reaction between the pair would be suitable for a dramatic 'slapstick' idea. In order to complete the composition it will need to end in confrontation or to be resolved so that one dominates the other.

Dance subject Characterisation

	Dance ideas	Analysis	Movement ideas
1	*Madame Défarge from 'A Tale of Two Cities' by Dickens* solo music: 'En Blanc et Noir' by Debussy (background)	Against a background of violence and tension there emerges a woman with a deep hatred driving her onwards to achieve her mission to destroy. She contains much evilness and moves in a sinister manner. Her constant knitting action is almost part of her as is the drop of the guillotine, a gruesome pleasure for her. She is a hunter and a killer. Among her own people she is a figure-head of the revolution	Main stress: body/quality. Thrusting and slashing actions involving jumping, travelling and turning contrasted with dabbing and flicking actions as part of a knitting motif. Direct cutting gestures of limbs, denoting guillotine movements, are contrasted with head rolling and swaying flexibly. Travelling could occur with firmness and directness contrasted with strong dynamic leaps of triumph
2	*A court jester* solo music: 'Lente-mente' from 'Visions Fugitives' by Prokofiev (background)	Music is a plaintive—a ring of pathos, but the character hides behind his façade of the fool, the idiot. He is a pro-moter of laughter. Trips, falls, oddly related events and rapid changes of mood often occur. Nothing seems constant. He makes a close relationship with the audience	Main stress: body/quality. Sudden jumps and steps and gestures of parts of the body, particularly in hands occur. Sudden contrasts of quality from flicking to pressing, dabbing to screw-ing or wringing, thrusts to floating actions. Rapidly altering phrase lengths could occur together with changes of level and direction
3	*A figure in Authority* solo	The character in authority can change from a leader, decisive and powerful to being authoritarian, marshal-ling, dictating and overpowering. A destroying force on self and others. A particular character could be chosen adding his or her personal characteristics	Main stress: body/quality. Upright carriage with firm, direct qualities in stepping and gesturing. Increases in tension and speed of movements could lead upwards, and then sink down in firm pressing or thrusting actions

Development of dance idea no. 1 with teaching hints

Discussion of dance idea

Information about the character of Madame Défarge can be found in *A Tale of Two Cities* by Charles Dickens. The History and English departments could assist with research, undertaken by the pupils, into knowledge of conditions at the time of the French Revolution. Book titles could be suggested by these departments for further research, reading into the causes of the Revolution and its effects on the French classes. The pupils could be divided into small groups, each group working on a different topic concerned with the French Revolution. A pooling of information would then follow and the character of Madame Défarge, as created by Dickens could be studied in the light of what is known about life at that time.

The class could then suggest possible ideas, examples of which are given in the analysis above, which describe the character of Madame Défarge and which perhaps give action quality words useful for stimulating movement ideas, for example, a knitting action could develop into the main motif for Madame Défarge's character. The guillotine dropping and heads rolling are other possibilities for dance motifs. Madame Défarge's personality, feelings and reactions need to be analysed by the class and transformed into movement ideas, perhaps stressing effort actions and the quality aspects of movement.

Work with movement ideas suggested by analysis

1 Use the knitting action as a stimulus for improvisations. Begin by suggesting that the action is mimed by the hands with each individual's attention focused upon the knitting movements of the hands and fingers. Then suggest that the movements are enlarged in size and in space, thereby involving more of the upper part of the body. As the action is repeated, draw the pupil's attention to the rhythmic content of the movements, the accented and unaccented parts. These need to be clarified and emphasised. The directions inherent in a knitting action need emphasising and extending to incorporate appropriate body actions. For example, a forward jab could develop into travelling forwards whilst jabbing with upper part of body, or an upward movement could develop into jumping, or a sideways movement into turning.

Gradually, an everyday movement serving some practical function is being transformed into a possible dance motif for a future composition.

2 Aspects of the knitting action can be selected and experimented with, for example, the rhythm of knitting could be performed in the feet and interplayed with the marching steps of the revolutionaries. Or the action of knitting could take place in areas of space other than in front of the body, such as behind or to one side or other of the body, invariably involving twisting and turning in the body. Or the action could begin above the head and with constant repeating travel down across the body.

3 The action could begin in the hands as normal, but rather small in size, and increase in size during repeats to involve the whole body in a knitting-type action. The action could begin close to the body and extend further away during repeats. Or it could begin in the hands and be repeated in the legs, then shoulders and head, or shared between two or more parts of the body.

Such situations give more possibilities to each pupil for discovering new movements for him or herself. The pupil should be awakened to a greater range of possibilities before selection for the composition begins.

4 Similar situations can be suggested for the action of the guillotine by the teacher or the students themselves, eg cutting gestures of arms or legs involving turning, or gestures of the head involving dropping, rebounding or rolling.

If such suggestions come from the class so much the better. If the class is not forthcoming then the teacher must try to place the class in situations which will lead onto others, such as the examples given above.

5 A study of the Revolution scene again could provide a fresh stimulus for other movement ideas. Examples such as marching rhythms and actions, triumphant leaping, thrusting attacking actions, storming in groups, whip-like slashing turns, and sustained, firm rising actions pressing upwards against an imaginary power may be improvised upon as relevant and possibly useful ideas for bases of dance motifs.

Travelling should occur as a contrast to the more static

work introduced earlier, in which case attention to floor patterns is necessary.

Playing and listening to the music at this point could well add another dimension to the pupils' creative thoughts. For there is indeed some triumphant marching suggested in some of the musical passages in the particular piece suggested for this dance idea.

6   Further travelling phrases could occur whilst working upon the determined actions of Madame Défarge hunting for her enemies, or stepping patterns which create a sinister quality.

Qualities of sustainment, boundflow and firmness could be used and contrasted with sudden stepping which is direct in quality.

It will help to use quality words to paint a more vivid picture for the class and stimulate the pupils' imaginations.

7   Ask the class to show any kind of movement which they consider to have a sinister quality. Using their ideas select some to show students their movements and point out how the qualities and shapes in the body as it moves can encapsulate the idea and esssence of 'sinister'.

The movements are in fact symbolising the concept of moving in a sinister manner. They are creating an 'illusion' of a sinister person.

8   Give the class every opportunity to contribute to further ideas on which to improvise so that a rich variety of movements has been experienced in readiness for selection at the composition stage.

Composition

1   Encourage, through discussion and with reference to improvisations above, each pupil to be fully involved and in tune with the character of Madame Défarge. Perhaps the solo to be composed may only use one aspect of the woman's character on which to concentrate. But it is important for the pupils to understand Madame Défarge as a product of the French Revolution as imagined by Dickens, and to come to grips with her as a person if the solo is to have depth of insight. Such understanding will govern each pupil's choice of dance motifs which she considers embodies the dance idea. Every solo should be quite different in personal style, form, ideas, motifs and so on, if the dance is truly a product of each student's imagination.

Encouraging individual styles to emerge and develop is an important part of sixth-form work. It is a part of dance teaching which is neglected and sometimes deliberately prevented from happening, and yet it is the very foundation on which to build an understanding of what dance, as one of the arts, is all about.

2   Suggest that the pupils select motifs previously improvised upon which have importance for them when considering the dance idea. For example, the knitting action could be used in such a way in the body as to appear more cramped, tense and jerky, reflecting the warped hatred within Madame Défarge herself. The jabbing action of the needles through the stitches could be transformed into an action of attack and intention to kill. The pulling of the wool over the needles could become a much longer, flexible movement, resulting in a slashing, jumping motif which sweeps all before it. Similarly the horror of the guillotine as it cuts, and the heads rolling, could be transformed into dance motifs.

3   Selected motifs need to be clarified by the pupils in use of body, shape in the air and on the floor, quality and dynamics. All these aspects will be used in such a way by each pupil, as to produce the kind of dance, the kind of aesthetic form each individual wishes to create because they see the end result as one which embodies *their* thoughts and ideas, feelings and reactions towards the character of Madame Défarge.

4   Once the dance motifs are clear, variations and development can be encouraged. Some pupils may have begun this in earlier improvisations or during clarification of motifs. Encourage phrases of varied lengths to develop, together with climaxes of varied intensity, thereby avoiding monotony of phrase length and size of climax.

5   Organisation of motifs and phrases needs to occur if a dance form is to be created. This involves relating one motif to the next, and so on, to create illusory forces and tensions which can be resolved in various ways.

6   If the music is used as background as suggested in the dance idea column, it should be used throughout the improvisations and compositional stages of the dance.

The pupils need to be very well acquainted with whatever piece of music they use with their dances, whether it be used in close relationship or as background (see chapter 8, page 172) so that they can use it in the most sensitive way with the developing dance. There may be passages in the piece of music which could highlight certain sections of the dance if both coincide in time. Some sections of the music may contrast with other sections of the dance, thereby creating a conflicting kind of relationship which may be the effect needed at that particular spot in the dance composition. Always, however, it is important to realise when using music with dance, the result must be an enriched dance not a piece of music enhanced by the accompanying dance.

7 The dance, when complete, should be performed in its totality a few times by each pupil—so that each has the opportunity of 'feeling' the form of the dance as a unified whole, and feeling the relationships created between dance form and musical accompaniment.

8 The class should be given an opportunity to critically appraise each other's work, in the light of certain criteria accepted by the group and with guidance from the teacher, for what they consider to be the essential elements of a satisfactory dance composition if it is to be judged a work of art. For example, does the dance give aesthetic pleasure? Does it have an inner logic throughout? Are there any striking motifs in the dance? If so, what makes them so?

Through discussion of this sort, the pupils can begin to appreciate dance as an art form, both from a spectator's and a creator's viewpoint, thereby developing an understanding for the process of making dances and the enjoyment and satisfaction achieved from so doing.

Dance subject   Moods

	Dance ideas	Analysis	Movement ideas
1	'Ennui' (boredom) a painting by Sickert	Limblessness, lingering nervous changing of position and distracted repetitive movements,	Main stress: quality/ relationship. Swaying, rocking, bound flow building up to impul-
	duo	eg foot tapping	sive movements on meeting; phrases build and die

Moods—*cont.*

	music: 'Gymno-pédies' by Erik Satie (background)		away with repetition and increases in tension
2	*Changing moods of adolescence* group body percussion	From depths to heights as insecurity gives way to arrogance; happy to sad; boredom leading to flippancy, clicking, snapping, stamping, cheering	Main stress: quality. Firm rising contrasted with fine-touch sinking and turning; monotonous repetition of a gesture gradually building to a bursting climax
3	*Lazy* solo music: 'Fables of Faubus' by Charlie Mingus (close relationship)	Drifting, sauntering deliberate affectations of laziness, eg lounging about, lethargic, drooping	Main stress: quality/body. Sustained dragging of feet and shoulder gestures, relaxed swinging from joints, eg hand-swinging, foot-swinging; exaggerated relaxed body positions

Development of dance idea no. 1 with teaching hints

Discussion of dance idea

Ask class to sit in a lazy position, show them the picture (Sickert's 'Ennui') in which figures look very bored, then request class to alter their positions to one of boredom rather than laziness. Discuss difference between the two; very relaxed for laziness while boredom contains a certain amount of tension, such as drumming fingers, a swinging foot, slightly awkward body positions. Try out these different movements and positions then proceed to other moods, for example, upright and tense for angry, upright but relaxed for happy, drooping shoulders and head for sad.

Work on movement ideas suggested by analysis

1   Class to start in their own bored position then to change to other positions but keeping the mood the same. Introduce music as they become involved.

> The music is used in the background to help create a suitable atmosphere.

2   Their movements are to be more deliberate—they may wish to exaggerate a gesture as they change position, or stress the quality of the movement, for example, a sustained quality with very light tension or a sudden much more powerful change.

> Each position should change quite naturally into the next; there will be moments of stillness then the change. The background music should help to keep phrases short and assist the flow of the movement.

3   As they change position, introduce a 'lifting and dropping', the body rising slightly as weight is shifted and then dropping to settle into a new position. Increase the lifting until the body is in a position to travel. The 'lifting and dropping' can be taken into a travelling, the body will be rising and sinking, different parts of the body having the initial movement which starts the phrase, for example, a shoulder initiates a rising forward travelling; then an elbow leads the sinking, perhaps turning. The whole of this phrase could be clearly structured, starting quite close to the ground with the 'lifting and dropping' motif which gradually builds up into travelling.

> The tension in the body will be quite light during the lifting but will be released to a great extent for the dropping.

4   At the end of a travelling phrase ask the class to come gradually to a finish—again holding a 'bored' body shape. Once more, change to other bored positions then, during a moment of stillness, one hand starts to swing from the wrist, this is an isolated movement which gradually increases then decreases in size. The tension in the hand may be varied from a light fine touch to a more firm touch. When the first movement has died down the other hand has a similar movement. The head is another part of the body which could adapt this isolated movement, followed, perhaps, by a foot. Ask the class to improvise with this idea, that is, the changing body positions and the isolated gestures.

> Bored people often do isolated unnecessary movements and this phrase is built up from such a movement.

5   The suggested background music—'Gymnopédies' by Erik Satie has a flowing rhythm which is very conducive to swaying.

From a sitting position, start the class swaying gently from side to side, build up the size of the movement then change the body shape. In some cases the body may be rocking from side to side on the hips, but if the top part of the body is important it will be swaying. In a standing position the body may sway from one side to the other or forwards and backwards, at times the head may be most important, or the shoulders, or the hips. Leave the class to improvise with this idea.

> Should their improvisations lack interesting phrasing, suggest ways of punctuating, for example:
>
> (i) Vary the degree of sway (increase and decrease).
>
> (ii) Use a turn to conclude a swaying phrase, so that the swaying increases and eventually spins or rolls the body into a different position.

Composition

1 The couple in the painting are bored—presumably with each other. It would be interesting to relate this idea to the composition. The relationship is quite sophisticated and should be treated as such.

> (a) The couple may start their duo as two separate solos, perhaps taking the starting position from the figures in the painting, and during the first phrases only the music and the mood will link them.
>
> (b) They may choose to dance similar phrases but at different times during their duo. For example, A starts with a rocking phrase, B dances the same phrase but part way through the dance; by this time A is dancing a different phrase (perhaps the phrase B started with).
>
> (c) The dancers could use the same phrase as each other but not exactly together; they may start at a different part of the phrase.
>
>> (i) One may be swaying forwards and the other sways backwards.
>>
>> (ii) One may be rising and the other sinking.
>>
>> (iii) One moving whilst partner is still.

2 Boredom means a complete lack of interest in what is going on. Therefore, whilst there is no obvious contact between the couple, they should be aware of the possible counter tensions (as in *1* above) and use them to shape their dance.

3   A chair could be used as a 'prop' (see the painting): it would
be possible to relate the movement ideas to a chair.
    (i) The swaying phrase could start from a sitting position.
    (ii) Changing positions when sitting on the chair.
    (iii) Rising and sinking leaning on the back of the chair.
4   The climax to the duo will not be very dramatic but could be
a short phrase danced together, almost accidentally, and perhaps
just a moment of stillness.

Dance subject   Greek mythology

	Dance ideas	Analysis	Movement ideas
1	*Icarus and Daedalus* duo music: 'Exodus' theme music from the film 'Exodus' (background)	Wing-like forms sweeping and hovering, surging upwards with exhileration; finally to melt and be dashed to the ground. Human frustrations build to disaster. There is the challenge to overcome man's limitations, tempting fate which is punished by death	Main stress: body/quality. Jumping involves gathering and scattering turns. Elevation plays a great part with or without jumping. Body shape changes from spreading to covering, disintegrating into a ball or elongated shape. Rising up contrasted with collapse and falling along the ground. Gliding actions increasing in tension could change to slashing and a thrusting drop. Wringing actions of despair may be used
2	*Plato's description of the nature of love in the 'Symposium'* (*Allegorical myth*) duo	An explanation is given for the attraction between man and woman in which the Gods create a man stronger than themselves with two heads, four legs and four arms. In order to reduce his strength they divide him into two halves each seemingly independent of the other. These half beings sense they are incomplete	Main stress: body. Pattern—making in the body—interplaying symmetric designs. One person closely related to the other in different ways, eg one behind the other, or side by side, or mirror image. Illusion of double image creating twice as many gesturing arms, legs and heads. Quality of firmness to create power and dominance. Crushing movements in wringing

Greek mythology—*cont.*

		and desperately seek their other half to unite again. This yearning for another is the fundamental of love	actions involving great tension are reduced in firmness to a fine-touch quality as partners separate and become two identities, each developing the former motifs in his own way. As partners are pulled closer so the tension increases in their movements and their body designs merge
3	*Orpheus in the Underworld* *A mythical version of deliverance attributed to his rites* Group or duo and group	Contrasting journeys related of Eurydice travelling to the dead followed by Orpheus charming his way in by playing his lyre. Writhing bodies of the damned are soothed by the music and changed to smooth and calm shapes. Fear of Hades resumed as the couple journey towards the light, firstly in confidence one behind the other, but gradually hesitation creeps over Orpheus and the couple face one another. Eurydice fades away to die again	Main stress: body and relationship. Variety of stepping, leaping, travelling with firmness and fine-touch and with sudden and sustained combinations. Curving gestures involving floating and gliding contrasted with wringing actions individually and in a group. Sequence of advancing and retreating in a duo stressing relationship of leader/follower and interplaying sudden and sustained qualities with moments of pause

Development of dance idea no. 1 with teaching hints

Discussion of dance idea

If the myth is not known by the class one would need to relate it and explain its context. Mythology is free from the constraints of reason and is fluid. Innumerable images can be created in mythological material, some are allegorical illustrating an argument or explaining a moral principle. One of the essential functions of myth was to minimise the difference between man and immortal. It was at one time a way of thought which created a world with which man could come to terms.

The Greek myth 'Daedalus and Minos' includes within its complexity the incident of Daedalus being imprisoned in the labyrinth with his son Icarus. To escape, Daedalus (an architect) builds two pairs of wings from feathers and wax. The story emphasises the desires of youth, a yearning to achieve the impossible—to fly, thereby breaking the bonds of human limitations. However, thoughtlessness results in Icarus falling into the sea. The story contains action, human aspirations and despair.

This dance idea could imitate the pursuit of a topic or project on Greek mythology or mythology of other civilisations including present day. The dance idea does not envisage a movement narrative taking place, but rather dances concerned with human aspirations and desires.

Work with movement ideas

It will be necessary to work in duos from the beginning since the two characters of Icarus and Daedalus are involved very much with one another. They are not so much contrasting as complementary.

1 Introduce turning movements of the whole body, full circle and part way round, on the spot and with travelling. Suggest kinds of turning with quality changes within the turning, such as spinning, rotating and screwing.

> Although variety in qualities will be worked on below in the initial improvisations, it helps the children to think in dance phrases rather than movement phrases if the teacher can use descriptive words such as 'screwing', 'twirling', and 'whirling'.

> The music could be played at this stage to create atmosphere for the children, and help towards the use of dynamics in their movements.

2 Suggest that weight is taken only on one leg as the body turns, and that the free leg and arms gesture thereby enhances the feeling of flight and turn. Repeat by stepping onto the gesturing leg and releasing the weight-bearing leg to gesture.

> Partners could stand near one another whilst they work independently.

> The gestures of the free leg and arms could play a major

part in creating an illusion of lift and suspension into the air even though the body is still grounded. Lifting the head and chest upwards also helps to create the illusion.

There is a tendency for arms to be used like 'aeroplane wings'—stuck out. It is the teacher's rôle to make apparent the various expressions which could be used to enhance the sensation of flight.

3 Experiment with the interplay between solid contact with the ground, tentative contact and no contact, first individually and then in twos, one partner supporting the other in elevating movements into the air, for example, travelling and being lifted around, landing, sinking only to travel and soar again.

Leg gestures should play an interesting part in creating shapes and patterns in the air.

4 Work on jumping sequences in twos which incorporate simple variation in size of jumps, changes of level, and increases or decreases of speed.

Repeated jumping actions give strong rhythmic phrases which need clarifying if they are to contribute to the structure and dynamics of the dance.

The chest area needs to be involved in rising and lifting movements if the sensation of elevation is to be achieved and become exhilarating. The chest could also counter-pull in a downwards direction creating antagonism towards the main statement of the body and perhaps expressing a feeling of apprehension and hesitation.

5 The relationship created between the two dancers should be the 'matter' of the dance. Various possibilities could be worked on by the class. For example, one of the duo (Daedalus) could dance protective and finding movements which are gentle, but which gradually become pulling and grasping movements, increasing in a feeling of urgency. The other partner (Icarus) could improvise on bold, powerful penetrating movements, which move away from Daedalus, spreading, rising and surging upwards, contrasting with phrases of wavering, hesitant movements during which the body may be contracted.

Constant reference made by the teacher to the myth should provide the couples with stimuli for ideas on human relationships with which to work. It must be made clear to the children that the purpose of the dance is not to tell the story of Icarus and Daedalus, but to reveal the children's responses to the human situations in the myth.

Mime could creep into the improvisary stage, in which case the teacher needs to encourage repetition of movements so that the rhythmic content may emerge, and to suggest that the children enlarge the movements in space and in their bodies, thereby using the whole body. They need to incorporate the body activities suggested, for example, a rising gesture could build to jumping, or an opening one to the side of the body could initiate turning.

6   Suggest to the couples that they work on a flying motif which they can build up into a phrase and which both dancers could perform in unison, alternating or overlapping, thereby creating interesting rhythmic interplays.

The teacher should try to encourage the giving of ideas from the couples rather than she herself suggesting alternatives.

By this stage the class should be more aware of shaping in movement and design in their duos, one dancer's body shape and design being complemented by the other.

Composition

The music needs to be listened to at this moment and used throughout this section of the work. A decision on what are to be the key ideas to the dance needs to be made.

1   Encourage selection and clarification of motifs so that they have clear body actions, body shape, air and floor patterns, qualities, rhythmic content and directions which encapsulate the key ideas around which the composition revolves.

2   Couples should be able to vary material using repetition of motifs and parts of motifs in which variations in quality, level, use of body and design can occur.

3   Development of material to involve new motifs, either by using parts of motifs previously stated or introducing contrasting material as a direct result of earlier motifs should be evident in the student's work.

This will result in longer dances of a more complex nature and form.

4   Shaping of phrases by building to climaxes and dying away from them, or ending phrases on a climax should appear without much mention from the teacher.

Punctuation of phrases using pauses, climaxes, hesitations should also be evident. Lack of punctuation results in wafting, endless movement which the teacher needs to correct with clear, well formed phrases, rhythmically structured and coloured by the textures and dynamics of movement.

5   Dances, at this stage, should have clear spatial aspects, a technically good performance, and clarity in effort content. The building and resolving of relationships between the dancers still need attention, for example, leader/follower, one static, one dancing, dancing in unison, and so on, bearing in mind that selection of certain relationships at a particular time in the composition is crucial to the artistic fulfilment of the dance idea.

6   Having composed the dance, suggest to the class that each couple performs their composition a number of times in order to perfect and master it.

The children gain much pleasure from just performing finished dances, particularly if they are their own compositions.

7   Give opportunity for the critical appraisal of other people's work by the couples studying each other's compositions, observing and commenting upon the aesthetic form and means of artistic expression.

The teacher needs to guide any critical appraisal being made if the skills involved are to be understood and mastered by the pupils.

Having devoted time and energy to their dances, some children can become highly sensitive to any kind of criticism about their work. It is important that aspects of the dance which were appreciated by the rest of the group are referred to and given credit by 'critics' in order to encourage further efforts into other dance compositions, and in order to encourage an independence to choose one's own dance ideas and to carry these ideas through to the completed dance form.

Discussion of choreographic problems, which various couples coped with and solved during the composing of their dances, could prove valuable for the group as a whole, each couple sharing in each other's experiences of the process of composition.

Chapter 7

Dance Ideas for 16–18 year Age Group

In the main, any inhibitions appearing in previous years should now have disappeared, although there will still be some pupils experiencing selfconsciousness in dance lessons.

A new zest for creative work often develops at this stage and is often met with enthusiasm and spontaneity—a mature attitude allowing the pupils to 'have a go', make mistakes, yet laugh at them.

When learning situations are presented to the pupils the creative aspect of choosing dance ideas should generally be stressed. Although dance subjects such as 'Characteristics of Primitive Dancing' are designed as a strong framework for pupils who have not experienced dance at all, or who are still uneasy in the open-ended situation; pupils who have followed a continuous course throughout their secondary education should experience a balance between creative work, studies and production work for performances. For some pupils, understanding dance as an art form is developing, not *just* enjoying the dance lessons as an artistic experience, which is also continuous. Aesthetic appreciation, if fostered, will play a part in a deeper understanding of the art form itself. Dance ideas should, therefore, incorporate sufficient richness of 'resources' or ideas in which the pupils can become mentally stimulated and involved. Sixth-form pupils seem to enjoy exploring their own and other people's fantasies, ideas and images, as well as other art forms such as poetry, painting, music, sculpture in which the artist's expression is embodied[4] in the medium of the art. All these can facilitate the pupils' understanding of what art is and how ideas and images can be transformed through the medium of movement and expressed in the form of the dance.

Dance subjects involved with human dramas and changes of mood may possibly prove interesting to sixth formers. Pupils will also enjoy selecting their own ideas and are quite capable of analysing them, especially those with a dramatic content. The children are also capable of discovering movement ideas to embody the dance idea.

The teacher selecting the dance ideas needs to use themes directly concerned with the pupils' life experiences. Also she needs to provide in her programme an appreciation of both lyrical and dramatic dances.

Sixth-form pupils, as a rule, enjoy group dances involving the whole class working to a common idea. In smaller groups clarity in shape and effort content can be seen during the improvisation stage and the pupils' work seems to resemble more closely the kind of dance seen in professional theatre performances. However, the teacher must remember that her task is to educate her class aesthetically through dance. Emphasis placed upon spectacular effects for performance purposes must be seen in perspective with the knowing and understanding of oneself and others through first-hand experiences incorporated in the creative works offered by the various art forms.

Individual work will tend to reveal further clarity in all aspects of movement and, towards the end of the sixth-form years, group work can achieve quite a high degree of clarity in form. Here the teacher needs to lay greater stress upon choreographic skills and the compositional stage as a whole when she is working from dance ideas. Real-life experiences need to be transformed and objectified in a dance form. Pupils need to understand that dance, like any other art form, is not concerned with *self* expression but with artistic expression—expression embodied in the art form. For example, if one wanted to compose a dance based upon anger one would not need to, nor should, feel angry whilst working on the dance. When we experience anger in real life the very last thing we wish to do is compose a dance as a means of venting our emotions. Art is not a copy of real-life situations but a transformation of reality—abstracted from reality to create something which did not exist before. Artistic expression requires abstraction using the imagination, and transformation using the materials available to the artist to embody expression in the medium of the work of art.

As a contrast and a balance to the programme, the teacher could offer opportunities to study classical art forms, such as

theme and variation, rondo, canon, and so on. A grasp, both intellectually and practically, of the process of development and the
action/reaction created within a dance can be developed from
such work.

Movement characteristics of 16–18 age group

From pupils who have completed a dance course throughout the
previous years one would expect a consolidating of the various
aspects of movement and a certain degree of overall clarity in the
work. Subtler movements and quality changes tend to be selected,
such as interplaying a flicking action with a dabbing one where
the fine-touch and sudden qualities remain unchanged but the
flexible quality of flicking changes to one of directness when
the transition to dabbing is made. Acquiring a feeling for balance between the whole body and small parts of the body
moving should have developed, together with a sensitive use of
large movements extending away from the body into space and
very small movements keeping close to the body centre. There
should also appear a balanced use of movement and stillness.
Punctuation of dance phrases can show quite a degree of sensitivity in some pupils' work, and climaxes are not always achieved
by leaping or rushing around vigorously.

The flow factor is often enjoyed by the pupils; particularly free
flow which utilises the enthusiasm and positive approach to the
work that the pupils seem to display.

Sixth-form pupils who have not danced before may show an
uncoordinated use of the body and much emphasis will need to be
placed upon body centre work and the initiation of central movements which the limbs may accompany.

Large group work is greatly enjoyed, as is the interaction of one
group with one or more other groups. The pupils tend to work
responsibly and actively as individuals and within a group. Most
pupils seem to participate rather than be carried along in group
work; perhaps because of their increased maturity and perhaps
because at sixth-form level the dance classes are often optional
and only those interested attend.

Smaller groups are capable of organising themselves throughout the whole compositional process.

Composition

Great stress should be laid upon choreographical forms and the movement content in a dance composition. Students should begin to show understanding and a basic technique in manipulating dance material and creating a 'seed' stimulated by the dance idea and germinating throughout the composition to give the dance unity and an inner logic of its own. This 'seed' or 'core' usually symbolises the most central aspect of the dance idea and may be one strong dance motif or the relationship created between two dance motifs. It needs to be impressive enough to influence further variations and development of motifs. An example of such a 'seed' in music is Beethoven's Fifth Symphony where four prominent notes command the whole work.

Although compositions are beginning to include more subtle changes of quality pupils tend to clutter their dances with unnecessary movements thereby masking the central theme.

Relationship is the key to composition and this can be understood by sixth-form pupils. Pupils should be aware of and exhibit in their dances various relationships—for example, relationships between two dancers or groups of dancers, relationships of one position to the next, one rhythm to the next, one shape to the next, and so on. It is important that clarity of the dance motif is emphasised in the pupils' work to allow for these relationships to be created and to become evident and possibilities fully explored by the pupils.

At this stage sixth-form pupils should begin to view their work in terms of its parts in relation to the whole. The teacher needs to help greatly in developing critical appraisal of the pupils' own dances, also of others, in terms of the illusion and transformation the dance achieves, the tensions created and resolved, the relationships arising from the placing of a dynamically strong motif against a gentle one and the comparing of that relationship with one created between two less dynamically strong motifs danced in succession. All these aspects may then be related to the dance idea from which springs the 'seed' of the composition.

It would be most beneficial for the sixth-form pupils to be given opportunities of seeing professional dance companies performing either in the theatre, or on film, videotape or television. A great variety of styles of contemporary choreographers needs to be presented. Visiting teachers who are authorities in particular types of dance could be used to give variety, width and depth of experience. Also, teachers from other departments in the same school, for example, Art, Music, English, could be invited to take classes aimed at widening the pupils' experiences and know-ledge of art and to assist their clarification of the concept of dance as one of the art forms.

Music

Again, as varied a programme in types and styles as possible. Some pupils of sixth forms do show a strong tendency towards dramatic music which is something for the teacher to foster, but this does need balancing with a lyrical content of work.

Whatever type of music is selected it needs to be the best of its kind wherever possible if it is to enhance the dance in any way (see chapter 8).

Dance subject   Characteristics of primitive dancing

(Suitable for beginners)

	Dance ideas	Analysis	Movement ideas
_1_	_'Breaking free from the force of gravity', lifting, striding and leap dances_ group: 5 or more music: drum accompaniment (close relation-ship)	Ecstatic motion in an upward or forward surge. A sensation of release from gravity into freedom. Flying upwards rebounding with joy and exhilera-tion. Complete involve-ment in the group to break the physical limitations of gravity	Main stress: body. Muscles of the body are stretched in degrees of extension followed by flexion particularly in the trunk and knee areas. Rhythmic stamping of even beats achieves ecstacy. Balance on toes gives place to leaping and skipping with chest and head focused upwards in elevating actions
_2_	_Breaking away from the force of gravity using swinging, swaying and suspending_	Swinging, swaying sus-pending sensations, hypnotic building to whirling and spinning. All dies down to calm-	Main stress: body. Movements start from a fixed point or centre of body around which swing-ing, rocking or rolling

Characteristics of primitive dancing—*cont.*

dances group: 5 or more music: drum accompaniment (close relationship)	ness and harmony. Urge to fly away from the earth with a feeling of weightlessness	starts. Pelvis and head important in accompanying rolling trunk movements. Gestures of limbs also accompany sustained movements, accelerate to sudden turning and spiralling. Rhythm of swings etc. ripple through body in contrast to a shifting of weight forwards and back building into leaping	
3	*Mimetic weapon dance* group: 5 music: drum accompaniment (close relationship)	Compels success in the fight. Attacking, dodging and darting for protection; defending, cowering, sudden recoil followed by lunging, throwing and striking out	Main stress: body/quality. Whole body extending into different directions from body centre. Movements swing forwards and backwards. Retreating movements contracting in centre of body. Steps and leaps combined with twists and turns of part or of whole body. Thrusting and slashing actions predominate contrasted with smaller dabbing and flicking actions in gestures of limbs. Moments of pause important. There is power in the group moving in unison

Development of dance idea no. 1 with teaching hints

Discussion of dance idea

The whole concept of the word *primitive* needs to be discussed, for there is primitive leading onward to civilisation, and primitive side by side with civilised, that is, culture. Exhilaration and ecstasy is the aim of the dance. To lose oneself in motor expression, to overcome the bodily limitations of man and break away from gravity are strong forces urging the dancers into rhythmic motion. Rhythmic motion has become 'the carrier and creator of almost every ecstatic mood of any significance in human life'.[5] These kinds of dance movements progress in rhythm and involve all parts of the body to move to each beat of the drums.

There is an existing logic in primitive dance forms which can be fully appreciated. There is a 'truth' to the dance idea in the movements in the dance. All primitive dancing seems to centre on leaving the human world to enter into life on a higher level. The physical self is lost and the mind is freed.

By the very way the rhythm of the movements tends to remove selfconsciousness in the primitive dancer so it seems to affect the sixth former in a similar way. Bodily awkwardness tends to be overcome in the compelling rhythms of the drums, which accelerate in speed influencing the calmer movements in the body occurring at the beginning of the dance to build up to an abandoned pitch.

Work with movement ideas suggested by analysis

1   Begin with leg and foot movements using stamping and bouncing loosely in joints of legs, varying the size of the movements and changing from moving on the spot to travelling within the stamping phrases.

> Many variations can be introduced on the simple stamping and bouncing movements, such as changing the level in which the body moves by bouncing low to the ground or higher away from the floor; or accelerating and decelerating the speed, or increasing and decreasing the tension in the body.
>
> Phrases of varying levels, and so on, need to be worked on from the start, so that pupils experience the different ways of building climaxes within phrases.
>
> Drum accompaniment needs to be played throughout to stimulate the body movements.

2   Work on whole body extending and relaxing into bouncing and stamping actions of legs and feet. Clarify and emphasise the accents in the drum rhythms by increasing the firm quality and relaxing again.

> Stamping involves thrusting actions where a great degree of firmness needs to be experienced in hips, legs and feet. Bouncing is more relaxed with less tension required and looser in the joints of the legs. The rest of the body 'jogs' in accompaniment.

3 Different stepping patterns on the floor can be made in which the whole body rebounds rhythmically to the strong leg actions.

The upper part of the body should be quite relaxed.

4 Gradually the surge upwards against the pull of gravity is introduced and the body weight is taken onto the toes whilst the body is thrown upwards and outwards into different directions. Gradually build the movements up until full extension in the whole body is attained and a contracting and relaxing into the centre of the body follows as a recovery and preparation for the next extension.

There is a difference between a contraction being made in the centre of the body and relaxing in the centre—the former being an active and possibly a forceful contraction of the muscles, and the latter a relaxing of them. Both movements could be explored.

The rhythmic aspect is of great importance as this is the compelling force to stimulate the desire to dance. The body and limbs echo each drum beat with their extending and flexing movements.

5 Ask the class what sort of movements suggest a fighting against the pull of gravity and the final breaking away.

It is hoped that the very simple dance idea is interpreted in the form of movements thrusting powerfully upwards and in leaping.

If the class do not offer such suggestions then the teacher will need to work on those suggestions given (if they encapsulate the dance idea). It is important that the pupils understand from this simple dance idea that some movement ideas are more suitable than others, and that creative work comes in finding the most unusual yet fitting ones.

6 Repeat the extended movements in stamps and rebounds by beginning the phrases of movement small in the body, perhaps only in legs and feet, and gradually increasing their size to involve the whole body reaching upwards, the chest and head looking up and the trunk arched backwards. Any gestures of limbs are also performed in an upward direction, thereby elaborating upon the chief dance statement made in the trunk of the body.

Stress the gradual increase in firmness achieved throughout the body.

This is also the beginning of motif forming and the building of dance phrases shaped with climaxes.

7 Repeat the previous movements, but finally break contact with the ground, and introduce skipping and leaping movements. Series of leaps could follow, growing in size and firmness.

Chest and head should be held 'open' and looking upwards.

Leaping is the main climax of the phrases. All is building up to the final break from the ground.

Leaping may need to be worked on from the point of view of legs thrusting upwards and the flow of movement travelling up through the trunk of the body to chest and head. Full extension of the body should be experienced at some stage.

8 Allow class to build phrases freely on the previous movements, varying the length of the phrases and the degree of climax; one could have four phrases each increasing in size of extension and firmness in the body until finally leaping takes over and the body ends back down on the floor.

9 Introduce a variation to the surging upwards, for example, surging forwards in striding movements. Movements could begin with a throwing gesture of legs which becomes stronger and larger, finally pulling the body into a surging forwards. Lunging gestures of arms or trunk, for example, could begin the phrase again, but perhaps as a contrast to developing into travelling; the lunges could extend away from the centre of the body into different directions penetrating space and then be drawn back towards the centre again, the climax made as the degree of extension into space reaches its fullest.

Again, a rhythm of lunge–rebound (recover and prepare)–lunge could be created and needs to be accompanied by pulsating drumming.

10 Using movements experienced so far suggest the class introduce variations on the same dance idea, for example, using one leg for balance whilst the other gestures in such a way as to express surging upwards. This could develop into a hopping phrase forwards and backwards, or in a circle.

Elements of composition are being introduced at this stage which will be built on in the next section when the dance form is created.

Composition

1 The dance idea is 'Break away from gravity'—a release from bodily limitations.

From the previous improvisations suggest each pupil selects movements she considers expressive of the dance ideas.

2 By repeating these selected movements clarity is achieved in the use and shape of the body and in the quality and rhythmic content of the movements. Try to encourage repetition in order to develop motifs expressing the dance idea. Repetition also allows variations on the original dance motifs to occur. Variations in degrees of tension, extension, speed and use of parts of the body can be composed, building them into phrases and shaping the phrases with climaxes.

3 Suggest groups be formed using motifs each member of the group has composed. Suggest that the group use unison movement and that they organise the motifs and repetitions and variations into an order facilitating the flow of movement from one phrase to the next.

A group dancing in unison can create a most powerful dance statement and group relationship.

4 It may be necessary to remind the group that there needs to be a major climax in the dance, for example, where the bodily limitations and physical laws governing the body are finally overcome through the dance. The problem of how this is expressed is for each group to solve, using the primitive characteristic movements to express the idea.

It is important for the pupils to grasp the vital point that, although in the lives of primitive peoples dance played a vital rôle (in that the forces of the dance were sufficiently real and compelling to those taking part as to involve them totally in the experience), contemporary dance is not about real forces but illusory forces. The dancer tries to create illusions through the medium of movement. Dance in our western culture does not play such a vital rôle in our lives.[6] It is hoped that by introducing the pupils to primitive dance they will experience something of those forces vital to the creation of the art form of dance.

Primitive-type dance movements also seem to train the body to move rhythmically and harmoniously, with the trunk and the centre of the body becoming totally involved in the expression of the movements, and the limbs echoing that expression in gestures.

Often the basic, compelling, rhythmic beat of the drums involves in dancing those pupils who have shown selfconsciousness in moving their bodies during other forms of dancing.

Finally, primitive dance tends to exhibit the rudiments of dance composition, uncluttered and unsophisticated, but nevertheless achieving the basic ingredient of the dance illusion—the freedom from gravity.

Dance subject   Bats

	Dance ideas	Analysis	Movement ideas
1	Poem 'Bat' by D H Lawrence solo music: *Kontakte* by Stockhausen (background)	Vivid images in poetry used to stimulate movement responses, eg twitching, twittering, creeping, shuddering, looping, dipping and diving, swirling creatures. Lumps flying in the air or hanging limp. Eeriness of unsuspecting, darting, flying movements creating skeletal shapes in the air	Main stress: quality/body. Bound flow quality with suddenness building to vibratory movements. Releases from this of free flow in rising and sinking may be used. Use of spine arching and twisting often whilst body balanced high on toes. Extreme changes of level can be used involving jumping with body spread or contracted. Gestures of all limbs play an important part
2	One's personal reactions to experiences involving Bats solo	Sudden recoil. Shivers and shudders in body. Sensation of creeping in one's scalp. Evil associations. Piercing tones and a flapping noise in flight. Unexpected dartings into different directions can provoke fear	Main stress: body/quality. Suddenness and bound flow predominate. Central contractions into retreating movements are contrasted with dabbing gestures into different directions. Movements of free flow leaping and diving act as a release from the bound flow quality
3	Primitive style Bat Dance	Bony shaped angular wings cling to body or spread to flap and	Main stress: quality/body. Rhythmic movements using arm gestures which

Bats—*cont.*

solo	shudder. Darting and weaving in unexpected	spread away from body and wrap around it;
music: vocal sounds and drumming	directions contrasted with body hanging limp sometimes upside down.	incorporate the qualities of suddenness and bound flow. Joints of arms stressed in angular design. Jump-
(background)	Small scratching movements contrasted with swooping and lifting	ing is used with body arching and bending, tipping over and suddenly dropping in thrusting actions which may be followed by flicking movements in extremities

Development of dance idea no. 1 with teaching hints

Discussion of dance idea

Copies of the poem need to be circulated around the group and read a few times. If possible, the poem should be given to the class before the lesson, so that the pupils are given an opportunity to become familiar with it. Practically, it may be necessary to use a number of dance lessons for analysing the poem and discussing its potential in terms of dance. This stage of the work should not be hurried, for the more one 'teases' or pulls out of the stimulus, the richer the range of possibilities will be for the future dance composition.

The poem under discussion has been selected as a stimulus for a dance composition because some of its poetic images contain clear action, mood and quality aspects suitable for stimulating movement ideas.

Suggestions for initial work on a dance composition could involve such ideas as selecting some of the poetic motifs. Each pupil needs to be encouraged to formulate ideas on a possible 'seed' from which the dance will grow and around which the composition will evolve. For example, the seed could involve the concept of an unobtrusive transformation from the flying swallows to flying bats (in the twilight), and the personal responses one had towards the two creatures could colour the qualities of the movements. Or one could become totally concerned with the concept of 'bat'.

Work with movement ideas suggested by analysis

1   Begin by suggesting that each pupil selects a phrase of poetry she finds stimulating for dance improvisation. The poetic image decided upon by each individual needs to be worked on, abstracting and transforming the image into a dance form and creating an illusion of events occurring. For example, 'flying madly', an image from the poem, would need work on creating an illusion of flying, and one would need to explore many and varied ways of flying using the whole body, parts of the body, and jumping and lifting movements.

> This learning situation is not only concerned with jumping but also with the sensation of jumping and of elevation. The body may not even leave the ground, but may only be involved with lifting and lowering movements and the illusion of being airborne.
>
> Help will probably be needed with the thrusting away of legs from the floor and the releasing of some tension in the body once it is airborne, stressing the chest and head areas to give a feeling of lift and flight.
>
> The music could be played at this point as it seems to echo the undulating rising and falling movements in the body.

2   Suggest that although only certain kinds of jumps and lifting movements will be selected for the final dance form, the pupils should explore all types of jumping and flying to give a greater range of movements from which to select those most significant and relevant to the idea of 'flying madly' (if this is the image they are working on).

> Jumping with turning could be suggested by the teacher, or hopping, skipping, leaping with height and length, exploring a variety of body shapes made whilst jumping or leaping into the air.

3   The 'flying' action is qualified in the poem by the adverb 'madly'. The illusion of 'flying madly' has possible connections with the qualities of free flow, firmness, suddenness and perhaps flexibility. Changes of direction, body action or level could also be incorporated into the movement patterns.

> Discussion could prove useful in the pooling of ideas at this point.

4   The improvised movements need to be repeated a number of times, changing the quality or shape, type of jump or rising movement, until each individual pupil begins to pare down the movements and a dance motif begins to emerge, embodying the kind of expression sought after by each pupil.

> Music could be played at this point to accompany the pupils' improvisations.

> It is important to encourage continuation of the improvisory stage for as long as possible, because the tendency is for the pupils to select dance motifs too early without prior sifting, sorting, seeking, exploring, rejecting and re-forming to achieve richer movement ideas from which to compose. One therefore needs opportunity to diverge during improvisation, and for some people this takes time.

5   Other images in the poem could be selected for work in a similar manner. A contrast to the previous image could be suggested, for example, 'Wings like bits of umbrella', but again action in the body will be needed first. In this case it may well be a gesture of limbs, in which joints and angles are emphasised and angular floor and air patterns explored.

> There is a tendency for the pupils to reproduce 'habitual' movements in their improvisations, which may or may not have relevance to the dance idea. The teacher needs to bring such movements to the notice of the individuals concerned so that they might judge the relevance and significance of these easily slipped-in movements.

6   If some classes are having difficulty selecting their own aspects of the poem on which to work, it may be advisable for the teacher to work the class together on one of the images (which she selects and directs). This will give the children a chance to experience the abstraction and transformation from the poetic image stimulus into the dance form and give a secure framework from which to progress towards their individual ideas.

> The teacher needs to bear in mind that there will always be some children who are not stimulated to dance by the material presented in the lesson, and it is for these children also that a more guided and directed beginning may initiate independent activity later.

7   Suggestions may need to be given to the pupils during selection of movement ideas from the poem. Such phrases as '... a

black glove thrown up at the light, and falling back' could suggest
a throwing action in part or all of the body, tossed into the air
with a limp quality and finger-like in body shape. Then the whole
falling backwards movement can be repeated if necessary.

> The teacher must emphasise the fact that the suggestions
> she gives are only one or two ideas, and that there are many
> more which the children could discover for themselves and
> which for them would be more satisfying.

> Music needs to be used in conjunction with improvisa-
> tions and suggestions from the teacher, as it will enhance
> the atmosphere and qualities within the dances.

Composition

1 It is advisable at some stage during the composing of the
dance to give an opportunity for the pupils to listen to and study
the music they are using. Although it is probably being used as a
background accompaniment to the dance, it needs to be brought
into the dance composition in a way which results in enlivened
dance, not music enlivened by the dance. If this is to be achieved,
then the pupils need to acquaint themselves thoroughly with the
form, rhythms, timbre, phrasing (in fact the general structure of
the music) so that they may use the music with their dance in a
way which enhances their own composition.

> This particular piece of music is not classical in its form,
> nor is it rigid, its rhythms and phrasing feeling seemingly
> irregular. It lends itself to a more flexible relationship with
> the dance form than would a Mozart minuet.

2 Suggest to the class that each person selects three possible
dance motifs from their previous improvisations, which they can
repeat to clarify for their own particular dance.

> If the pupils have further difficulties in choosing motifs, the
> teacher will need to stipulate which possible ideas they
> could work on to create dance motifs.

3 Suggest that the selected motifs are repeated, varied and built
into simple phrases.

4 Encourage development of material which will eventually
result in new material being incorporated into the dance composition.

The moment for introducing new material into a composition
is a significant one for the form of the dance. One has to be wary

of introducing new material and new ideas into a composition too soon, before other motifs have been explored sufficiently for the expression to be fully embodied in their form.

> It is so easy to end up with a string of unrelated fragments of dance phrases each with its own individuality and expression, but each lacking in any relationship with the next one because there had not been any growth of expression from one to the next. Ideas need to grow and develop through the dance motifs into phrases, sections and finally the dance form, until the overall artistic expression is complete.

5 It is important that the teacher allows each individual to work at her own pace, and in her own way, to create a completed dance form unhindered by any pressures to complete the dances quickly or to produce compositions which are pleasing to the teacher herself. The dance is about a 'bat' and how each person has responded to the stimulus in dance terms. It is each person's unique contribution, their own work of art, which matters, not whether the end products satisfy the teacher's own preferences for style, and so on.

It seems to be one of the most difficult tasks for a dance teacher to critically appraise a child's composition without introducing her own preferences into the set of criteria for assessing the dance.

6 Encourage the class to perform their finished compositions several times in order that they have an opportunity of 'feeling' the form of the dance now it is complete. Changes may need to be made in the dance, such as shortening or extending sections because the balance of phrase-lengths in some parts does not feel smooth to perform.

The children should begin to recognise in their compositions an inner 'logic' which may break down in some sections. The more experienced teacher can often see such sections and is in a position to point these out and give guidance to help the pupil improve the composition.

7 Give opportunities for those pupils who want to perform their dances to the rest of the class to do so, but avoid forcing any unwilling children. The teacher needs to make it quite clear to the class that they are watching one another's work with a view to developing their aesthetic appreciation of dance, and developing the skill of aesthetically and critically appraising the

composition by drawing up for themselves a list of criteria they consider a dance must satisfy if it is to be called a work of art.

They should be encouraged, whilst watching their classmates perform, to voice their likes and dislikes, to criticise the relationship between the dance and the music, and then to find reasons (which are aesthetically grounded) to support their views. A discussion on any relevant issue could ensue and could prove very valuable to the development of the pupils' abilities to aesthetically appreciate dance and to critically appraise it as an art form.

Dance subject   Money

	Dance ideas	Analysis	Movement ideas
1	'*Money*' solo music: by Pink Floyd from their album 'Dark Side of the Moon' (close relationship)	A working action gradually interspersed with a 'piling-up' action, the piling becomes compulsive and piles are built in all directions. This horde is protected by barriers and tension grows but compulsive 'piling' takes over once more	Main stress: body. Body and rhythm in a working action, eg typing, bricklaying, followed by a 'piling' motif, hand gestures pile one over the other starting low with a sudden quality all around the body to incessant rhythm, broken as special barriers are formed the links spreading to surround piles
2	'*Cash*'—*a poem by D H Lawrence* trio	'Vicious competition' which gradually increases in violence, contrasted by the harmony of a 'goal-bird', 'gaoler', and 'strolling outside in fear' relationship in which tensions are still there but not so obvious	Main stress: relationship. Firm gestures confronting partners whose reply is equally aggressive; slashing punching answered by pressing, wringing; the 'gaoler' makes spatial barriers around the 'gaol-bird' who has restricted movements; the rich man has a restricted pathway 'a narrow beat'
3	*Attitudes to money—spend-thrift and horder*	A light-hearted exaggeration of avarice contrasted with abandoned 'spender' as they vie	Main stress: body. Limbs spreading from centre with light and firm touch, very flexible, swirl-

Money—*cont.*

duo	with each other for dominance; one very earnest in attitude, the other much more playful	ing, jumping, rhythmical spreading hand gestures; contrasted with grasping, enclosing gestures, sucking into the centre, turning the body, a firm direct enfolding of one side of the body across the other, travelling on a direct pathway
music: 'Money Makes the World go Round' sung by Liza Minelli from 'Cabaret'		
(background)		

Development of dance idea no. 1 with teaching hints

Discussion of dance idea

Many stories exist of greed and misers having hoarded money devoting their lives to working for and acquiring money without spending. The lyrics of the song 'Money' by Pink Floyd clearly state the selfish attitude of many people in this respect. However, many young people today despise the acquisitive nature of man. Discussion along these lines should prove interesting. It is also important to discuss the actions used when working and when counting money and how it is possible to build them into a dance motif by the use of rhythm, repetition, and perhaps altering some aspect of the action. Listen to the music.

Work on movement ideas suggested by analysis

1 The music is very rhythmical; included in the beginning is the sound of a cash register. Suggest working actions for the class, such as typing—exaggerating the hands and body in the up and down action and then tilting the body sideways as one arm pushes the typewriter across; or, working a cash register, including the sudden forwards and backwards movement of the cash drawer; further examples are digging and bricklaying. Trying out their chosen action to the rhythm of the music will help to phrase their action.

Repetitive actions like bricklaying are easiest to build into dance phrases. Explain to the class that they are taking the action and changing it into a dance motif by using rhythm, clarifying the quality of the action (for example, light touch for typing, firm touch for digging) and and making the spatial patterns interesting, not necessarily copying the real action.

2   Once work has been established then the money rolls in. A piling action, using the rhythm in the music starts close to the ground and short sharp hand movements, one on top of the other, gradually rise higher in building a pile. As soon as one pile is built another starts to grow. Piles vary in height and grow all around the dancer. One hand may build one pile whilst the other is building a different one—either both together or alternately. The whole body should be involved in the action, sinking low and slowly rising watching the piles as they grow.

> The even stress of the rhythm of the music helps to keep the action repetitive and it can become quite obsessive.

3   A greedy, grasping action follows, fingers reaching out and circling over to come back towards the body, wrists very prominent. This strong curling over passes through the whole of the body; legs also join in, the feet reaching out with toes grasping and knees with strong curving gestures going into any area of space around the body. These actions should be developed into a motif, for example, one hand starts with a small slow grasping gesture, the other hand follows with a larger quicker grasping gesture. Then both hands at the same time reach out with an expansive grasping gesture, starting with an impulse which gradually dies away as the arms return to the 'centre', while slowly turning the body.

> The grasping action is quite strong and flexible with an innate impulse which builds up tension within the body appropriate to the dance idea.

4   Misers protect their money. In dance the body can form barriers, spreading out first in one direction then another with a quality of firmness. The space patterns will be very clear as direct lines are drawn by the limbs reaching away from the centre of the body, wide gestures skirting around the space the body occupies and other pathways which cut diagonally through the centre of the body. A barrier may be built up from the ground with the body rising and spreading or, as the body turns, barriers may cross each other.

> Make it clear that the spreading starts from the centre of

the body and there will be some return to the centre in order to commence another 'spreading'. This 'spreading' motif should be developed into a phrase in which 'barriers' are built and it will contrast spatially with the previous 'grasping' phrase which is much more flexible.

5   The class should now improvise to the music using earlier phrases and motifs as they choose. Possibly they will start with their working action, but this is certainly not the only way to start a dance on 'Money'. Ask class to continue to work alone until they have chosen and developed clear phrases (it will probably be necessary to fade out the music as it goes on for some time).

Composition

1   The music is bound to be influential as it starts with the rhythmicised sound of a cash register and goes on to a repetitive phrase. However, it is not necessary to be influenced by the lyrics which might prove difficult to hear clearly. If lyrics are to be used in the dance idea these can be found written on the record sleeve.

2   The dance could express an opinion about money, each dancer deciding whether she needs to introduce other motifs to express her ideas. For example, motifs involving spending money, throwing it away, perhaps burning it, or even motifs expressing how she feels about money. Happy to have it! Desperate without it! These additional ideas together with the previous work should be the basis of composition.

3   At this age the group should be aware of their own contributions to their composition and be encourged to experiment with motifs, breaking them down into smaller fragments of other motifs to give more complex dances. They may change the qualities of the motif, for instance (a) the strong curving gestures of the 'grasping' phrase could gradually become lighter in tension, almost playful, and gestures could then float freely through the air turning the body lightly, or (b) the 'piling' phrase could be sustained instead of sudden, giving a completely different sensation, one of piling up forever.

4   Their completed composition may not be an obvious expression of the dance idea—in other words, the dance idea has not limited them but stimulated them to try out various ideas and then to use the material in their own way for their own dance.

Dance subject   People

	Dance ideas	Analysis	Movement ideas
	'People' a poem by D H Lawrence group music: 'Us and Them' from 'Dark Side of the Moon' by Pink Floyd (background)	Advancing, menacing, closing in to a focal point, then passing each other travelling in a distinctive way; together at first then splitting group, finally crowding together again overpowering	Main stress: relationships. Contrasting pathways in space and contrasting body shapes. Rhythmical travelling on diverse pathways, direct, meandering etc, clear body shapes, curved, angular etc, leg gestures and held arm positions
2	*'Les Saltimbanques' by Picasso* (blue period, circus figures) group	Isolation within a group very little reaction to others, a feeling of pathos and hopelessness, bound together by a performance but separated by a feeling of being withheld and alone	Main stress: relationships. Group can spread away from starting position and also move as a unit, but pathways rarely cross as each member dances her own solo act, clowns, balancers, strong men, etc, involving exaggerated gestures with a quality of bound flow
3	*'Melting Pot'* group music: by Blue Mink (close relationship)	An interpretation of the lyrics of the music involving movements developed from mime, eg 'take a *pinch* of white man', and later a 'Mick Jagger Walk' for 'Mick and Lady Faithful' Chorus danced as a group study in a circle everyone in unison in the 'Melting Pot'	Main stress: relationship/body. Rhythmical mime actions flowing from one to the next, eg first verse hands important in 'pinch' 'wrap' —a dabbing for 'add a touch' these lead the body into dipping and rising for 'Red Indian Boy' then a curling action around the head and folded for 'Yellow Chinkies'. The whole group comes together for chorus with a stirring of the whole body starting low to high, the arms taking an important part

People—*cont.*

> both together in front of
> body with a circling
> movement ending in
> spinning and a gather-
> ing together of the group
> as everyone ends 'coffee
> coloured'

Development of dance idea no. 1 with teaching hints

Discussion of dance idea

Read the poem and discuss the idea D H Lawrence has expressed. He likes 'people . . . quite well at a little distance' and views them objectively, looking for differences. He prefers to be alone as he likes to feel 'there is room enough in the world'. Discuss how these ideas might be interpreted in dance. Group relationships could illustrate the distance he likes to keep from people and how people pass each other in a different way. The end of the dance could be concerned with overcrowding.

Work with movement ideas suggested by analysis

1 Travelling diagonally across the room, leaping out with one foot after the other, legs stretching forwards, arms swinging easily at the side to reach towards the corner easily.

> Feel the regular rhythm, the strong thrust of the feet and the resilience necessary on landing.

2 Vary the movement above by changing the rhythm, for example, two long leaps, three shorter leaps—repeat.

> Ask class to work on a different rhythm of their own.

3 Still on a direct pathway diagonally across the room and with the same 'eager' quality, but this time first one side reaches out towards the corner, then the other side, with steps in between and arms gesturing high towards the corner one after the other—this is the type of movement seen in American dance, such as in 'West Side Story', and covers a lot of ground in a short time.

> Pupils should respond well to these steps as they will recog-
> nise them from the cinema. Encourage them to speed across
> the room in a very determined way.

4 Each pupil should work on her own variation of the steps above, perhaps changing the rhythm or the gestures, including a turn or introducing rising and sinking.

> Stress individuality, going back to idea from the poem of 'aloneness alive in them'.

5 In contrast to the previous idea, travel across room on a meandering pathway with the body moving in a very flexible way, turning, rising, sinking, bending, arms and legs gesturing in a flexible way too. Build a motif with a clear rhythm, for example, first one side of the body rises then sinks, then the other side; the pathway will be curved, the phrase finishes on a turn on the spot, starting low finishing high (repeat).

> There is a clear difference from previous phrases as arms and legs indulge in space—this can be freely flowing and smooth, or gestures more angular and flow more bound. Again, once the phrase has been introduced leave the class to improvise and devise their own phrases.

6 A further idea on travelling is a hesitant pathway involving advancing and retreating then advancing again (repeat). This can be taken on a direct or curved pathway—the front, side or back of the body leading. Arms and legs may have important gestures within the phrase, for example, travelling, initiated by a forwards movement from the 'centre' of the body, both arms reaching forwards at waist level, then a pull back from the back 'centre' to retreat with arms lowering (repeat).

> There is an 'ebb' and 'flow' in this phrase and a clear rhythm will be built up. Again, the class should improvise with the phrase, turning will add a variation.

7 If background music is used, introduce it now as the class improvise with the clearly different ways of travelling.

> During improvisation ask the class to be aware of what the others are doing as they pass. There should be variety, some people taking the direct pathway, passing others using a meandering pathway, and the hesitant people surging forwards and backwards.

8 (a) Introduce a slow start, gradually speeding up, ending in a sudden stop. (This can be incorporated within the phrases already used.)

(b) A sudden start, gradually slowing down to a slow finish.

> For a sudden stop and a very slow finish it is necessary

for the class to feel a bound-flow holding back the movement.

(c) Advance towards a partner either stopping suddenly or finishing slowly. Dance this with a menacing quality, watching partner carefully, getting very close together before stopping.

Each partner should use a different phrase to advance, eg one with leg gestures important; her partner may advance sideways. Again, utilise phrases developed earlier.

9 Still with a partner, very close together, use a shuffling of feet and a nudging of shoulders to crowd one another out, turning around each other, ending with one partner towering high over the other who has sunk into a small area at her partner's feet.

This is an idea for jostling for 'room left in the world'. The body will be held with firmness, any gestures necessary will be strong. There is a menacing quality as each person strives to gain space in the world.

Composition

1 The class has already been working on the composition of the dance and should have some ideas to express the poet's feelings about 'People' in a group dance of five or seven, each person expressing their own individuality, going their own way and crowding one another out, for example:

(i) 'At a little distance' they could create distances in space between one another, starting close together then spreading away.

(ii) Show 'distance' by starting away from a focal point then all closing in on that point.

(iii) 'I like to see them passing and passing
    And going their own way.
    Particularly if I see their aloneness alive in them.'

The group could find their own individual way of passing each other using their own earlier improvisations. Group shapes will grow—maybe a tight group which then spreads away from each other. There will be differences in levels as they pass. Some members of a group may travel together at one stage, relationships occurring which are brief in time but which help to add form to this part of the composition. Floor patterns will be very important—there will be crossing pathways, converging pathways, parallel pathways, and some will wind around others.

(iv) 'Yet I don't want them to come near'. Clashes and repulsions could happen in the group as they turn against each other, or the group could choose a focal point towards which to advance together and be repelled as a group.

(v) 'If only they could leave me alone
    I could still have the illusion
    That there is room enough in the world.'

A jostling of the whole group as they nudge each other with their shoulders, weaving around each other, feet shuffling, getting into a smaller, tighter group until eventually one person sinks and the rest of the group tower over her, crowding her into a small space.

2   The group may decide to follow the poem through as described or they could have the poem read aloud as they dance, with suitable long pauses as the dance takes place. If background music is required Pink Floyd's 'Dark Side of the Moon—Us and Them' would be suitable.

3   Their interpretation of the poem may be in other ways—they may have enjoyed the different ways of passing and wish to base their choreography on this. In this case they may stage their dance with some going 'off stage' leaving only a few dancers 'on stage' at a time. They may 'pass' each other singly, each person having an individual motif. The numbers in the group passing could gradually increase until at the end of the dance the whole group is able to express the last idea in the poem—'The illusion that there is room enough in the world.'

Chapter 8

Music for Dance

Dance–music relationship in the theatre

Throughout their histories, music and dance have been wedded. In the theatre the audience expect the traditional bondage between the two arts to be confirmed. Audiences come to the theatre to be entertained. They come to hear the music that the dancers dance.

In life, sound and movement usually occur simultaneously. We expect one as a by-product of the other. We use sound to give information about movement and vice versa. We recognise the significance or meaning of an event by our observations of movement and perception of sound. Because of our intuitive response to the combination of sound and movement, we attempt to make relationships between music and dance. This is the tradition imposed upon the teacher of dance working in the field of education. Most dance choreographers, today, seem to believe that the two arts, dance and music, belong together, and music is certainly the art form most readily used by the teacher for stimulating and accompanying the teaching of dances.

Although the choreographer and the dance teacher both work with the art form, each has a different aim in view, and one which music serves to fulfil. It is also an aim in which, if the choreographer is to call his performance dance and the teacher to offer a unique aesthetic experience worthy of a place in the school curriculum, the result of the collaboration between the two arts must be enlivened dance.

The dance in the theatre is a spectacle through which the artist communicates to his audience in as vivid a form as possible. It is in fulfilling this aim that the choreographer uses music with the dance to enliven and enrich the spectacle. If the dance relies heavily on the structure and form of the music, it will become dependent on the musical form for its expression, and the result will be enriched music like the early music visualisation of the nineteen twenties. If the dance can assimilate the music into the whole illusion then the spectacle is one of enlivened dance.

In education, however, dance is used by the teacher to educate the children in the aesthetic, and in so doing develops their faculties to the full by providing them with an aesthetic experience from which their understanding of the art form of dance is enriched, and the understanding of themselves and their environment is deepened through first-hand experience. These artistic experiences can only come about if the children are given the opportunity to create dance forms or works of art, however crude, and are equipped with the skills to master the disciplines of the art, and to form aesthetic judgments and critical appraisals.

The dance teacher will often use music to help her in this task which must surely be to produce enriched dance improvisations and enlivened dances, and aesthetically more vivid experiences. Her aim, like the choreographer's, is not to produce enlivened music but enlivened dance. For the nearer the children get to producing the art form of dance, the greater becomes their understanding in the world of artistic expression.

Throughout this book emphasis has been laid upon the teaching of dance as an art form providing the children with an aesthetic experience. It should be possible for the development and extension of what happens in the dance lesson in schools to lead naturally into the professional work of dance companies in studios and theatres, although it cannot be emphasised strongly enough that it is not the aim of the dance teacher to train her class in becoming professional dancers. She should, however, be handing down to the children some part of their cultural heritage, and instructing them in the skills and techniques necessary for keeping their culture viable. The mature art form in the theatre should provide a reference point for the dance teacher, as it is the dance in the theatre that seems consciously to provide an aesthetic experience for the onlooker. It is also dance in the theatre that seems to need music not only because of tradition, but also to facilitate communication and expression in the dance. Music by its very nature supports and enhances the dynamic image, the dance[6]. It helps the dancers to sustain the primary illusion of dance, that is, virtual powers or forces which pull the dance this way and drive it that way, forces which build and resolve, ebb and flow, forces which are not of this physical world but are created by the choreographer in the medium of his art[6].

The communication between choreographer and audience is strengthened by the collaboration between the music and the dance.

In present-day theatre, contemporary dance choreographers have varying views on the nature of the dance—music relationship. MacMillan [7], for example, worked very closely with the music because he felt he needed the musical support for his dances. As he admitted: 'I don't think I could write dance quite independently of the music.'

Nikolais, on the other hand, composes music for his choreographies that gives an impression on the ear which is in keeping with his dance spectacles and enlivens the performance. He finds the kind of music that is most enlivening and that does not impose structural limitations upon the dance form is electronic music, with its droplets of sound, jingle jangles and strange whines. He also creates the dance without accompaniment, thereby finding the performance rhythms that work best, and only when the dance is assembled and rehearsed does he include the music. The result seems to be one of an enriched dance atmosphere.

Nikolais, is unique in that he is both choreographer and composer and is therefore in a position to understand the demands made by both arts upon each other. For the balance between the restrictions imposed by one art and the demands made by the other is only achieved in the hands of a choreographer who is acquainted with both art forms, as indeed Nikolais seems to be.

In recent years the tendency has, however, been for dancers and musicians to combine forces—each drawing upon his expertise in the hopes of creating a true collaboration between the two art forms. The ideal situation for the choreographer is to commission a musical score for the dance. The dance can be partially or wholly complete before the musical score is composed, or the two art forms can evolve side by side but independently of one another. Few choreographers can finance such a process or, if they can, find willing musicians to collaborate with them. The small dance companies have to be content with 'ready-composed' music piped, or played live, for the dance performance. The tendency is for the music to have a corseting effect on the dance by subjecting the dance to the principles of musical composition. The result is often a contrived dance.

In the past, music has tended to serve the function of synchro-
nising the movements of the dance, articulating time by emphasising the beat and clarifying the measured time of the motion
which coincides with that of the music for the dance. This illus-
trates Cage's opinion that modern dance seems to depend upon
musical structure because it lacks a clear rhythmic structure and
a clarity of phrasing. He sees rhythm as the very life structure
which, as such, is rarely clear in modern dance. He says that when
a modern dance choreographer has followed music clearly in
musical phrase structure, the dance has tended to be clear in
phrase structure also. He feels that the practice of choreographing
a dance first and obtaining music later tends to result in the
choreographer being concerned with things in the dance other
than clarity of rhythmic structure, and its appearance later when
the music has been included has been accidental and isolated.
This has led to a general disregard for rhythmic structure even
when the dance is composed to music already written; the result
is lack of clarity of expression in the dance.

If dance and music are to extend in their inter-relatedness into
an art form, then their relationship must be based on a much more
organic unity and one which allows each fullness of expression.
This implies an inseparable growth throughout a composition of
the two forms. It relies on working relationships between music
and dance, and between instrumentalists and dancers. One notable
example of a working relationship between choreographer and
musician seems to be that of Cunningham and Cage. They simultaneously compose dances and music to exist as two aspects of the
same totality. The enlivened dance is achieved as follows: Cage
attempts to make music structured by chance devices and is thus
freed from his imagination and harmony. By a similar method
Cunningham structures sequences of movement. The result of
the collaboration is two activities going on at one and the same
time, in the same place for the same length of time. A complex
pattern evolves from the two activities simultaneously performed,
which are essentially different. The dance becomes the prominent
feature enlivened by the music because Cage composes the kind
of music that consists of sound and rhythm stripped of 'the cum-
bersome top heavy structure of musical prohibitions'[8]. Such
music akin to percussion becomes readily available for Modern
Dance. The materials of dance already include rhythm and with

the addition of sound become rich and complete in vocabulary. Cage suggests that when the compositions of the dance and the music occur simultaneously and together, the materials used should be worked together. 'The music will then be more than an accompaniment, it will be an integral part of the dancer' [8]. The sound will have its own and special part in the composition as a dance element.

Whether the music enlivens the rhythmic structure of the dance, or the mood or dramatic qualities in the dance, the collaboration which exists between the music and the dance must be such as to result in an enriched dance not an enslaved one. Cunningham [9] expresses this sentiment when he says: 'The support of the dance is not to be found in the music but in the dancer himself on his own two legs, and occasionally on a single one.'

If dance rests heavily on music for structural support the result is not a dance enriched and enlivened, but a dance corseted and contrived; and it does not seem possible from the examples given earlier for the two arts to exist, in the collaboration, each as art in its own right. It seems that a work of art in one art form can serve in the making of another work in another art form. Whatever the procedure whether the music be composed alongside the dance composition or a 'ready-made' piece of music used, the dance choreography must be the work of art which predominates if the result is to be a dance work of art in its own right, and the music must serve in the making of the dance. As an onlooker, one experiences a situation where one's eyes are absorbed with the activity, and the musical sounds are accommodated into the primary illusion of the dance.

This process of assimilating one art form into another is clearly explained by the chief exponent of the theory, Suzanne Langer, in her book *Feeling and Form* and is a subject too detailed for this chapter. However, the principle of assimilation does reflect on the teaching situation when the questions of how to use music in dance teaching and what music to use arise.

Dance–music relationship in education

Much of what has been written about the dance–music relationship in the theatre is relevant to the dance–music relationship in the dance teaching situation. The chief problem the teacher faces is how to use music so that it does serve in the making of a dance. This is also one of the chief problems the choreographer has to face. But where the end product for the choreographer is a spectacle, the end product for the teacher is an aesthetic experience achieved by making a dance which will educate each child in the same 'valuable' way.

The dance teacher is faced with many problems when using 'ready-made' music which has not been composed specially for the dance. She, like the choreographer, has to solve problems of varying lengths of dance and music, differing lengths of phrases of each, the creating and resolving of tensions in each may occur at different times and for different reasons, the placing of accents and so on. The solving of such problems is often achieved by distorting the musical forms rather than assimilating their elements into the dance form. So much music is stretched to fit the dance and is abruptly ended irrespective of the completion of musical phrases. Sections of music are often extracted from various compositions and strung together to form an accompaniment for the dance without regard for composer's style, period of musical piece, musical intention or key.

If the music and dance can evolve side by side in the teaching situation as in the theatre, many of these problems would not arise. Some dance teachers are fortunate in obtaining a pianist who can achieve this, but for the majority of teachers this luxury is not available and the only alternatives are to use 'ready-made' music or to liaise with the music department (which can result in the children composing their own music for their own dances and vice versa).

One big danger when using 'ready-made' music is for the teacher to compose a dance study or whole choreographed dance for the children to master, and then to look for a piece of music which will fit in with the dance structure, form and rhythms. This is an almost impossible task to fulfil, and one which often leads to distortion of the musical form. If one is going to use music with a dance idea one needs to select the music before the dance idea has been developed and formed, and allow the dance to grow alongside the musical form. The teacher must be very careful of the danger of squashing the dance composition into a structure which conforms to the accompanying musical one. This practice does not result in enlivened dance but in the kind of dance and music relationship which Humphrey[10] believed to be unnecessary and false. For she felt that the two arts are such different media that the dance could only be damaged by being cut to fit every phrase, every beat and measure of the music. Moreover it was a redundant practice because the composer had said it all once, so why repeat it in movement terms? Humphrey evolved a theory of relating dance to the music while leaving each its individuality intact. This results in a dance and music partnership in which neither dominates nor dictates the other, in short, a true collaboration.

The key idea here seems to be *leaving intact each form's individuality*. The dance idea and the using of the music should be worked side by side during the process of the dance composition but sometimes concentrating on one, and sometimes on the other, but never concentrating on one to the exclusion of the other.

When faced with all these problems concerned with the use of music in dance teaching, one may well question the use of music at all. Dances can and should be from time to time composed without any accompaniment. It is important that the children have this kind of experience in which they can become more sensitive to concentrating totally on the medium in which they are working and shaping to produce an art form.

From the examples in the theatre one can appreciate that music is used with the dance to give another dimension to the dance composition. Likewise, children composing dances should not be denied the use of music to enrich their dances. But in order to enrich their compositions they need to be taught the skills necessary to understand and use the piece of music they are working with. For example, music can add the dimensions of clear rhythmic structure which the dance on its own tends not to achieve. Children's dances, particularly, lack phrasing and breathing spots or, in short, punctuation. Using music in their dances can give the needed clarity of rhythmic structure.

The flow of music will often carry children onwards in motion, and the dynamics of the music will have great influence upon the dynamics in their dances, for example, a piece of music containing strong pulsating rhythms can provoke strenuous stamping and pulsating body movements giving rise to most exhilarating and ecstatic sensations. Some of the early primitive dancers used drumming in a way in which strong flexing and extending of legs and trunk were accompanied by vibrant drum beats.

It is very difficult to sit still to the beating of drum rhythms, to strong rhythmical music and, almost certainly, in discotheques. Pulsating rhythms played loudly and endlessly in an enclosed space attract crowds of young people to dance.

Children of any age in schools are no exceptions to this, and love to dance to music. It is left to the judgement of the teacher to strike a balance between dances in silence (where the ebb and flow of the dance may develop unhampered and the natural rhythms of the dancers may be created in movement phrases free from musical interference), and dances enhanced by accompanying music setting a mood for the dance or rhythmically creating patterns with the rhythms of dance or relating dance phrases to musical ones, dynamics to dynamics, climaxes to climaxes, and so on, to achieve a dance composition enriched by the music elements assimilated within its form.

Although there are these advantages with using music to help children compose rhythmically clearer dances, children can become dependent upon music for providing suggestions for the next dance phrase and the overall form to their dances. They tend to look to the musical form for resolutions to the problems in the dance composition, with the result that the logicality of the dance form is suspect and transitions clumsy or abrupt because variation and development of dance material had not grown from the evolving dance form, but from the completed musical form.

To help the teacher in her tasks of selecting and using music for dance we have, therefore, categorised the ways in which music can be used. The categories depend largely on the nature of the relationships created between the music and the dance idea and dance form.

There seem to be two broad categories. Either a piece of music can be chosen as a dance subject stimulating the dance ideas, or it can be selected to support and enhance the dance ideas. In its enhancing role the relationship created with the eventual dance composition may be closely binding or loose. When a loose relationship is created we have termed such use of the musical accompaniment as 'background use'. The dividing line between 'close relationship' and 'background' can be very thin and depends largely upon the degree of influence the structure of the music has upon the structure of the dance. For example, when composing dance studies one often works in close association with the rhythmic structure and phrasing of the music selected to accompany the study. But the rhythmic aspect of the music could also be used in a 'background use' to influence the rhythmic aspect in a dance motif inspired by a poetical image. In each case the musical rhythms are influencing those of the dance, but in the latter example, this may be the only structural influence the music has on the dance, and the dance form would be loosely related to the music by this rhythmic element.

When music is used as a dance subject stimulating dance ideas and, from these, movement ideas, it can suggest some kind of action, style, quality or mood. The relationship realised between the music and the dance ideas evolved by that piece of music would be different for each person, and in each instance may involve one aspect of the music influencing the dance more than any other. An example of this is in the first-year lesson guides where carols are used to stimulate rhythmic stepping patterns within the form of the round dance. Such rhythmic effects as syncopation and counterpoint can be achieved between the musical and dance rhythms, or the resultant dance performed without the musical accompaniment.

The mood of the music often stimulates dance ideas, the textures and dynamics of the music seemingly evoking emotional responses in the listener. Musical ebbs and flows, tensions building and resolving seem to arouse in us certain surges of feeling and emotions which build and resolve, ebb and flow also, and this kind of stimulation can be the starting point for a dance. In the fourth-year lesson guides, one of the 'Sea Interludes' from Britten's opera 'Peter Grimes' has been used as a direct stimulus for a dance idea, 'Storm at Sea', the music evoking vivid illusions of turbulence, wrenching, tearing and clashing. 'Sounds of Silence' has been used in the 14–15 age-group lesson guides to stimulate the composing of a dance study, the qualities, mood and phrasing of the music having special influence on the movements selected for the study.

When comparing the use of music such as the 'Sea Interludes' with that of 'Sounds of Silence' it can be seen that although both directly stimulate the dance ideas, they are two very contrasting pieces of music in style, form, structure, orchestration and so on, and the dance compositions and study will also require contrasting styles, movement techniques and choreographic skills in composing them. The 'Sea Interludes' is thickly orchestrated, large in sound and dramatic. The 'Sounds of Silence' is thinner in orchestration, simpler in structure, softer in sound and lyrical. It would be very difficult to work as closely to the rhythms of the 'Sea Interludes' as one could with those of the 'Sounds of Silence'.

When music is selected to enhance a dance idea already decided upon, it can (as stated earlier) provide a background accompaniment for the dance, thereby creating a loose relationship with the form of the dance. Or it can support the dance form in a much closer-knit relationship, the music perhaps influencing such aspects of the dance as phrase lengths, rhythmic or dynamic content, mood or overall shape of the dance.

Music, as a background, can sometimes create a relationship with the dance in which the music gives one aspect of the dance idea and the dance contributes another to 'complete the picture'. This kind of relationship can sometimes be created with dance ideas based on characterisation where one side of a character may be worked on in the dance, whilst a contrasting side may be suggested by the music. See, for example, dance subject 'Characterisation', in the sixth-form lesson guides where one of the dance ideas is concerned with the characterisation of a clown figure, the dance movements being involved with outward joviality, the will to please others and make them laugh and with the exhibitionist. Meanwhile the music of Prokofiev, 'Lentemente' from 'Visions Fugitives' adds a note of pathos, thereby creating a contrast with the dance figure but contributing to the full expression of the dance.

The kind of music most suitable for 'background' use tends to be atmospheric, loose in structure and more irregular in phrasing and rhythmic content. A minuet by Mozart would be too binding and rigid in its structure, rhythms and form for background use.

Selection of music for dance in education

So far only the ways in which music could be used have been discussed. There still remains the problem of which music to select for what dance ideas and for which age groups.

The first point is to select short sections of music which are in themselves complete. Dissatisfaction results when music is abruptly ended in the middle of a musical phrase because the dance form has been completed.

A second point to consider when selecting music for dance teaching is the nature of the group of children for which the dance lesson has been prepared. For example, many teachers will often select thickly orchestrated and atmospheric music for a first-year class in an attempt to sweep the children into dance. Much of this kind of music is complex in structure and orchestration and so large in sound that the children tend to become overwhelmed, confused and are happy to sit and listen rather than be stimulated to dance. In fact there are many pieces of music, in which the work is fully developed complete in its significant expression and the musical form closed. These are usually the great musical works, such as Beethoven's symphonies, which do not give up their musical forms easily and are therefore best not used.

First-year children tend to enjoy clear rhythmic music with simple phrasing and easily discerned orchestration and melody, for example, Saint-Saëns's 'Carnival of the Animals' or Walton's 'Façade'.

Second-year children seem to enjoy and understand similar music to first years but perhaps also that which is stronger in dynamics, and with a strong element of drama. For example, the accompanying music for the dance idea 'Witches' Sabbat', 'Symphonie Fantastique' by Berlioz, under the dance subject 'Witchcraft'.

Some third- and fourth-year children are beginning to develop certain inhibitions towards creative work in dance classes and problems of stimulating them to dance seem to increase. The peer group culture is also growing in influence, and conformity to this is of paramount importance to many third- and fourth-year children. 'Pop' music is enjoyed by most children of these age groups and so is 'pop' dancing. For this reason 'pop' music has been introduced to fourth-year groups in the dance subject 'Pop Star'.

Some presentation of dance material for third- and fourth-year classes is in study form so that the adolescent groups may be helped through this difficult period of learning a creative subject such as dance. The relationship between dance study and musical accompaniment or stimulus is close, both musical style and movement being selected for their potential appeal to the third- and fourth-year groups; an example being 'Zorba's Dance' in the third-year lesson guides.

Primitive drumming is selected for third-year groups to give an opportunity for the captivating, exhilarating rhythms to evoke rhythmic body movements in the children. It is hoped that by becoming absorbed in the drum rhythms these children, feeling inhibited when dancing, will overcome their inhibitions. For it is very difficult to keep still whilst the compelling drum beats are being played.

The 'Sea Interludes' mentioned earlier are used in the dance subject 'The Sea', and are included for use with fourth-year children who enjoy dramatic group dances and who enjoy working creatively, as some will from time to time throughout the year. They also provide a contrast with the pop music of the dance idea 'Popular Dances of the Past'.

Fifth- and sixth-year lesson guides show examples of music from classical to 'heavy pop'. The range in orchestration, style, period and form should be as wide as possible and liaison with the music department in the school could result in talks about composers and their music.

Fifth- and sixth-form pupils should, if they have followed a dance course throughout their secondary education, begin to show signs of working with autonomy on their dance compositions, selecting their own dance ideas under a given dance subject perhaps, and even choosing their own musical stimulation for dance ideas or musical accompaniment to support a dance idea. There may be situations where the teacher has selected and used a piece of music as a teaching aid in a particular learning experience and finds that after a period of time working with the music the initial stimulation has gone, and the music is having a limiting effect on the pupils' work. An example of this is given in the fifth-year lesson guides under the dance subject 'Clowns' in which the music of Scott Joplin is used. In practical teaching situations it was found that this kind of music provided a strong initial stimulus which was later found to have too corseting an effect on the developing aesthetic form of the dance. The music was discarded at this stage having provided valuable enrichment for dance and movement ideas.

Electronic music can be used in sixth-form work, particularly because of its 'looseness' in rhythmic and harmonic frameworks providing the unexpected droplets and jingle jangles of sound. It can create an eerie strangeness to a dance when used as background to enhance the dance expression, and its relationship with the dance is sometimes created by simply existing together at the same time.

Sixth-form dances tend to be more complex in form, but the pupils' understanding of musical form seems not to match this degree of complexity. There is therefore an important role for 'mood', such as some electronic music or tone poems; music to play in accompanying these dances as a background.

It can be seen how necessary it is for the dance teacher to become acquainted with a 'library' of music which could be useful in her work with all age groups throughout the secondary school. In structuring the lesson guides which use music for one reason or another, we have attempted to include examples of music from a variety of composers and ages. Examples have been given which are also easily available to the teacher. The pieces of music used in the lesson guides have, therefore, been listed below and an indication of the ways in which they could be used with dance ideas has also been suggested.

Age group	Composer or performers	Music	Use	Dance subject
11–12	Saint-Saëns	'Fossils' from *Carnival of the Animals*	Direct stimulus	Fossils
	Honneger	*Christmas Cantata*	Background	Christmas Dance
	Vaughan Williams	*Fantasia on Christmas Carols*	Background	Christmas Dance
	Hely-Hutchinson	*Carol Symphony*	Background	Christmas Dance
	Traditional	*Carols*	Close relationship	Christmas Dance
12–13	Holst	'Neptune the Mystic' from *the Planets*	Background	Creatures
	Berlioz	'Witches' Sabbat' from *Symphonie Fantastique*	Background	Witchcraft
	Soundtrack from *Butch Cassidy and the Sundance Kid*	'Raindrops keep falling on my head'	Background	Weather

Age group	Composer or performers	Music	Use	Dance subject
12–13 —cont.	Borodin	'Polovtsian Dances', Section 3 from *Prince Igor*	Close relationship	Weather
	Mussorgsky	'Gnomus' from *Pictures at an exhibition*	Background	Creatures
		'Listen and move' records, a suitable electronic piece	Background	Witchcraft
13–14	Stravinsky	*Rite of Spring*	Background	Violence
	Bernstein	'The Rumble' from *West Side Story*	Close relationship	Violence
	Bernstein	*Walk on the Wild Side*	Background	Pop Star
	Santana	*Abraxas*	Background	Pop Star
	Pink Floyd	'Time' from *Dark Side of the Moon*	Background	Pop Star
	Primitive	Drumming	Close relationship	Primitive Style
14–15		Theme music from *Zorba the Greek*— 'Zorba's Dance'	Direct stimulus	Zorba's Dance
	Joni Mitchell	'Circle Game' from *Ladies of the Canyon*	Close relationship	Growth
	Ravel	*Bolero*	Close relationship	Growth
	Simon and Garfunkel	*Sounds of Silence*	Direct stimulus	Sounds of Silence
	Britten	'Four Sea Interludes' from *Peter Grimes*	Background	The Sea
	Traditional	Jazz (Charleston)	Close relationship	'Popular' dances of the past
	Any	Olde-tyme Waltz	Close relationship	'Popular' dances of the past
	Any	Rock-n-roll	Close relationship	'Popular' dances of the past
15–16	Debussy	*En Blanc et Noir*	Background	Characterisation
	Prokofiev	'Lentemente' from *Visions Fugitives*	Background	Characterisation
	Scott Joplin	*The Entertainer*	Background	Clowns

Age group	Composer or performers	Music	Use	Dance subject
15–16 —*cont.*	Schumann	'Pierrot' from *Carnaval*	Background	Clowns
		Theme music from *Exodus*	Background	Greek Mythology
	Satie	*Gymnopédies*	Background	Moods
	Charles Mingus	*Fables of Faubus*	Close relationship	Moods
	Any	Loud-brass-band	Background	Clowns
16–18	Pink Floyd	'Us and Them' from *Dark Side of the Moon*	Background	People
	Blue Mink	*Melting Pot*	Close relationship	People
	Stockhausen	*Kontakte*	Background	Bats
	Pink Floyd	'Money' from *Dark Side of the Moon*	Background	Money
	Liza Minelli	'Money makes the World go round' from the film *Cabaret*	Background	Money
	Primitive style	Drumming (live)	Close relationship	Characteristics of primitive dancing
	Primitive style	Vocal sounds and live drumming	Background	Bats

References in the text

1 Goethe, Johann Wolfgang von: *An essay on man.* In *Great writings*, New York, New American Library, 1977.
2 Laban, Rudolf: *Modern educational dance.* London, Macdonald and Evans, 1975.
3 Preston-Dunlop, Valerie: *A handbook for modern educational dance.* London, Macdonald and Evans, 1969.
4 Reid, Louis Arnaud: *Meaning in the arts.* London, Allen and Unwin, 1969.
5 Sachs, Curt: *World history of the dance.* New York, Norton, 1963.
6 Langer, Suzanne: *Feeling and form.* London, Routledge and Kegan Paul, 1953.
7 MacMillan, Kenneth, quoted in Percival, John: *Experimental dance.* London, Studio Vista, 1971.
8 Cage, John: *Silence.* London, Calder and Boyars, 1968.
9 Cunningham, Merce, quoted in 8.
10 Humphrey, Doris: *The art of making dances.* London, Dance Books, 1978.

Many of the poems referred to in the text are included in the following two anthologies:
Baldwin, Frances, *and* Whitehead, Margaret: *That way and this.* London, Chatto and Windus, 1972.
Wain, John: An anthology of modern poetry. London, Hutchinson, 1967.